The Four Seals of the Dharma

Lama Khenpo Karma Ngedön

The Philosophers collection presents Buddhism's fundamental ideas in the form of short, clear themed works. It makes the necessary elements for informed knowledge of Buddhism according to the various traditions accessible.

The Four Seals of the Dharma

Lama Khenpo Karma Ngedön

With a Preface by Professor Sempa Dorje

Translated from the French by Jourdie Ross

The Philosophers

RABSEL
Éditions

ORIGINAL TITLE : Les quatres sceaux du dharma

©Rabsel Editions 2018

Special thanks from the English translator to Marjorie Erickson.

RABSEL PUBLICATIONS
16, rue de Babylone
76430 La Remuée, France
www.rabsel.com
contact@rabsel.com

This project was supported by the DRAC and Normandy Region under the FADEL Normandie, France.

© Rabsel Éditions, La Remuée, France, 2021
ISBN 978-2-36017-029-6

Table of Contents

Table of Contents

Preface by Professor Sempa Dorje

The venerable Khenpo Ngedön has published a teaching today on the four seals of the Dharma or the four receptacles of all the Buddha's teachings. It constitutes the foundation of the Dharma of the texts and explains the negative actions it is necessary to give up and the positive actions it is necessary to adopt.

I rejoice profoundly in the excellence and perfection of this work!

It specifically focuses on the impermanence of all things and the fact that all conditioned, samsaric phenomena are suffering. It also describes the meaning and benefits of renunciation and the realization of liberation—the perfect state—thanks to the noble path.

These explanations are remarkable and adapted to the present era.

Therefore, I profoundly rejoice in this admirable

work and appreciate it to the greatest degree possible, for it is truly excellent!

We can read in one of the sutras:

Of all footprints, the elephant's are outstanding;
Just so, of all subjects of meditation for a follower of the Buddhas, the idea of impermanence is unsurpassed.

The Buddha also said:

For a practitioner, thinking of impermanence constitutes the root and the source of all Dharmic thoughts.

I hope that, in the future, Khenpo will continue to publish teachings on refuge, mind training, etc.

The sun of the refuge welcomes all those who trust in its luminous warmth.

For the intelligent and the wise, all phenomena are important.

Even harmful emotions are useful to practitioners who have experience of realization.

For those who aspire to liberation, no phenomenon is senseless. Each has its importance.

By turning our minds toward the Dharma, every thought becomes a Dharmic thought.

When we become aware of impermanence, if we experience remorse upon realizing that we are not putting our life to good use, this will take on its full meaning.

By recognizing our attachment to samsara, renunciation is born.

By observing our lack of diligence in practice, we renounce Mara.

For all of these reasons, this little book will show you the path to follow and turn your mind toward the Dharma—without a doubt, intelligent reader! I make wishes and prayers that this be the case!

May the most excellent virtue increase!

Sempa Dorje, January 31, 2015

A Warning to the Reader

This book is not intended for the individual who seeks happiness through sensory pleasures in this life alone. This teaching is for those people on a quest for nirvana and an authentic practice to reach it. Therefore, I have particularly focused on the reflection concerning impermanence and renunciation of samsara. These two notions constitute both the point of departure and the essential strength of the journey to nirvana for sincere practitioners who wish to enter this path.

The term renunciation indicates the necessity of renouncing the creation of causes that inevitably result in suffering. This is the path that the Buddha and the authentic masters of the past followed and applied.

During the teaching that I gave in Vic,[1] due to a lack

---

[1] This book is the result of teachings given by Khenpo Ngedön at the Buddhist center Karma Txöpel in Vic, Catalonia, Spain on May 26 and 27, 2012.

of time, I was unable to cite sutras and *shastras* or to explain them in detail. I preferred to give a rational presentation of the topic—in other words a logic-based one.

To dissipate the doubts of readers who may ask themselves if qualified masters taught renunciation and impermanence and if they are truly necessary to reach nirvana or enlightenment, I offer several complementary, trustworthy sources here.

In *The Sutra on Establishing Mindfulness*[2] it is stated:

> *In samsara, you will never find*
> *Even an ounce of happiness.*

The Buddha also said[3]:

> *To meditate persistently on impermanence is to make*
>   *offerings to all the Buddhas.*
> *To meditate persistently on impermanence is to be rescued*
>   *from suffering by all the Buddhas.*
> *To meditate persistently on impermanence is to be guided*
>   *by all the Buddhas.*
> *To meditate persistently on impermanence is to be blessed*
>   *by all the Buddhas.*
> *Of all footprints, the elephants's are outstanding;*
> *Just so, of all subjects of meditation for a follower of the Buddhas, the idea of impermanence is unsurpassed.*

---

2   sangs rgyas bcom ldan 'das. *dran pa nye bar gzhag pa bzhi bstan pa,* [*The Sutra on Establishing Mindfulness*]. Biollet: Kundreul Ling, Undated.

3   Patrul Rinpoche, Padmakara Translation Group. *The Words of My Perfect Teacher* [*rdzogs pa chen po klong chen snying tig gi sngon 'gro'i khrid yig kun bzang bla ma'i zhal lung zhes bya ba zhugs so*]. Boston: Shambala Publications, 1999, P. 54.

Maitreya[4]:

> *Just as there are no good smells in a cesspit,*
> *There is no happiness among the five classes of beings.[5]*

Guru Rinpoche:

> *It is said that in this samsara there is not as much*
> *As a pinpoint's worth of happiness to be found.*
> *But should one happen to find just a little,*
> *It will contain the suffering of change.[6]*

Jetsün Milarepa:

> *In short, without awareness of death*
> *All Dharma practice is useless.*

The master of Mahamudra, Gampopa, said:

> *The suffering that leads to disgust for the cycle of existences*
> *must be seen as a spiritual master.*

Nagarjuna:

> *Accumulating wealth, protecting it, and using it is exhausting.*
> *So understand that it is the source of endless problems!*

---

4   Patrul Rinpoche, previously cited Footnote 3, p.137.

5   We count five states of existence (instead of six) when not distinguishing the demigods from the gods.

6   Patrul Rinpoche, previously cited Footnote 3, p.137.

Gyelse Thogme Zangpo in *The Thirty-Seven Practices of Bodhisattvas*[7]:

> *The practice of all the bodhisattvas is to leave behind one's homeland,*
> *Where our attachment to family and friends overwhelms us like a torrent,*
> *While our aversion towards enemies rages inside us like a blazing fire,*
> *And delusion's darkness obscures what must be adopted and abandoned.*
>
> *The practice of all the bodhisattvas is to take to solitary places,*
> *Avoiding the unwholesome, so that destructive emotions gradually fade away,*
> *And, in the absence of distraction, virtuous practice naturally gains strength;*
> *Whilst, with awareness clearly focused, we gain conviction in the teachings.*

Atisha:

> *So long as you have not established stability*
> *Distractions will harm your practice.*
> *Abide in the solitude of forests and mountains.*
> *Far from disturbing activities, you can thus fully devote yourself to Dharma practice,*
> *And at the moment of death, you will have no remorse.*

---

7 Zangpo, Gyelse Thogme. "The 37 Practices of Bodhisattvas." Lotsawa House. https://www.lotsawahouse.org/tibetan-masters/gyalse-thogme-zangpo/37-practices-all-bodhisattvas. December 3, 2019.

Manjushri's teachings on mind training, called Freeing Oneself from the Four Attachments, state:

> *If you are attached to this life, you are not a Dharma*
> *practitioner.*
> *If you are attached to the cycle of existences, you are not*
> *a renunciant.*
> *If you are attached to your own benefit, you have not*
> *manifested enlightened mind.*
> *If attachment persists, you are not endowed with the view.*

The Four Dharmas of Gampopa constitute a concise instruction for practicing Mahamudra:

> *Grant your blessing so that my mind may become one with*
> *the Dharma.*
> *Grant your blessing so that Dharma may progress along the path.*
> *Grant your blessing so that the path may clarify confusion.*
> *Grant your blessing so that confusion may dawn as wisdom.*

In *The Supplication to the Past Lineage of the Mahamudra*, the Kagyü master Bengar Jampel[8] also says:

> *It is taught that detachment is the legs of meditation.*
> *Accord the great meditator who has cut off the bonds of*
> *this life—*
> *Without desire for food or wealth—*
> *The grace of indifference to gain and honor!*

---

8   Zangpo, Bengar Jampel. *Sgrub brgyud rin po che'i phreng ba kar+ma kA tshang rtogs pa'i don brgyud las byung ba'i gsung dri ma me dpa rnams bkod nas ngag 'don rgyun khyer gyi rim pa 'phags lam bgrod pa'i shing rta* [*The Supplication to the Past Lineage of the Mahamudra*]. Biollet: Kundreul Ling, Undated.

We can also cite *The Chapters Stated with Intention*[9]:

> *All that is living is impermanent and disappears at*
>   *the moment of death;*
> *All that is accumulated is impermanent and ends by*
>   *dissipating;*
> *All that is composite is impermanent and ends by separating;*
> *All that is built is impermanent and ends by collapsing;*
> *All that rises is impermanent and ends by descending;*
> *Friend and enemy; happiness and suffering; good and bad;*
> *All thoughts that cross the mind—everything is*
>   *impermanent.*

In short, if we truly want to obtain stable happiness—
profound inner tranquility; perfect peace—we must
take great care of the causes that lead to it:

Ethical humanism.
Nonviolence.
Contentment.
Confidence in the law of karma and the Three Jewels.
Moral ethics.
Impermanence.

These elements give meaning to our lives and are essential for accomplishing all spiritual practice. Without
them, it is difficult to attain nirvana.

When we abide in a nonviolent state—*ahimsa*[10]—hostil-
ity around us ceases.

When we speak only truthful words, listeners adopt
our point of view.

---

9   Sangs rgyas bcom ldan 'das. *ched du brjod pa'i tshoms (Udānavarga)* [*The Chapters Stated with Intention*]. Publisher Unknown, Undated.

10 *Ahimsa* means nonviolence in Sanskrit.

The precious gems of positive qualities accumulate around those whose honesty is unshakeable.

If we respect moral ethics, *shila*,[11] in all circumstances, we obtain spiritual strength.

Supreme happiness is the fruit of contentment.

When we trust in the law of karma and we respect it, our life goes from positive circumstance to positive circumstance.

When love and compassion bloom within us, all beings are dear to us.

When we develop pure thoughts, we purify that which is harmful.

The Buddha said:

> *Give up harmful actions;*
> *Practice virtue tirelessly;*
> *Cultivate a balanced state of mind;*
> *This is the Buddha's teaching.*

---

11 *Shila* means moral ethics in Sanskrit.

Prologue

Lord,
Clothed in a saffron robe, luminous
As the setting sun,
You incarnate natural peace and noble ethics.
Always considering others—
Guide of people, you turn the wheel
Of the excellent teachings concerning
Emptiness and interdependence.
Supreme Instructor!
Incomparable Muni!
Buddha!
Filled with trust, I pay homage to you.

An Invitation to the Reader

It is important that readers of this teaching have the appropriate motivation—the wish to apply the teaching in order to attain enlightenment and thus become capable of benefitting beings by helping them liberate themselves from suffering.

Introduction

The four seals of the Dharma represent the essence of all of the Buddha's teachings. The explanations given here are short. Nevertheless, the meaning they express is as vast as it is profound. Furthermore, it is invaluable.[12]

Shakyamuni Buddha committed to the path by generating *bodhicitta*—the wish to attain enlightenment in order to accomplish the benefit of all beings. He followed

---

12 Khenpo Ngedön gave this teaching during the month known as *saga-dawa*, which roughly corresponds with the month of June in the solar calendar. Khenpo Ngedön gave the following explanations, "This is the most important period of the Buddhist calendar. During this month, we celebrate the birth, enlightenment, and death of the Buddha. It is said that if we accomplish virtuous actions during the day of the full moon—the fifteenth day of each month according to the lunar calendar—the benefit that these actions bring about will be multiplied by one hundred. Furthermore, if we carry out such actions during the month of *saga-dawa*, the benefit is one-hundred-thousand-fold and will have even greater reach. Therefore, we can recognize this opportunity, rejoice in it, and—conscious of this good fortune—exert ourselves to follow the teaching with joy and enthusiasm."

the path by accumulating merit and, in the end, he realized enlightenment—the state of Buddhahood.

Once he had attained enlightenment based on his immense compassion for beings, he turned the wheel of Dharma three times. He transmitted three cycles of instruction, which make up a total of 84,000 teachings. The four seals sum up the essence of these teachings.

We consider ourselves Buddhist, but what does this expression mean?

Atisha said that a person who takes refuge vows toward the Buddha, the Dharma, and the Sangha is a Buddhist. Thus, a Buddhist is someone who affirms the Three Jewels.

There are two differences between a Buddhist and a non-Buddhist.

- One difference relates to conduct or behavior (taking refuge falls into this category).

- One difference relates to the point of view regarding phenomena.

Manifesting love for all beings and practicing generosity is not ethical conduct exclusive to Buddhism. Many people of different convictions adopt this ethic—from a religious and non-religious point of view. We can, therefore, speak of a general or common conduct in this regard.

The specificity of Buddhism lies in the practice of generosity and of beneficial acts for others based on refuge in the Three Jewels—the Buddha, the Dharma, and the Sangha.

Regarding the point of view, we can distinguish two types of individuals:

- Those who accept the four seals (which we will

explain in detail in the current text) can be called Buddhist.

- Those who do not accept or do not act in accordance with the four seals are not authentic Buddhists, even if they refer to themselves this way or wear monastic clothing or other identifying articles.

Study and understanding of these four seals are therefore essential.

In the world, we can distinguish those people who choose to follow a spiritual path from those do not follow any form of spirituality.

Furthermore, among those individuals who adopt a spiritual path, we can distinguish two types:

- Those who believe in the existence of a creator god.
- Those who do not accept the principle of a creator.

Today, those who believe in a creator god generally belong to one of the following four religious groups:

Christianity
Hinduism
Islam
Judaism

The religious traditions that do not accept a creator god include, notably:

The Samkhya school of India. This is a very ancient tradition including a school of thought that still exists today.

Jainism.

Buddhism.

With the exception of Buddhism, all religions affirm the existence of an inherent and independent self. Buddhism is the sole religion or philosophy that does not accept the reality of a self independent of any other factor.

Buddhism adopts the perspective of both the dependent origination and the emptiness of all phenomena. As such, no phenomenon exists solely based on itself in an independent fashion. This is also referred to as the absence of inherent existence. The teaching on the four seals of Dharma explains this point of view.

Today, there are various ways of defining a Buddhist and numerous criteria that contribute to those definitions. Nevertheless, we can sum them all up with the following sentence: whoever accepts and applies the four seals of the Dharma is Buddhist.

This teaching shows the Buddha's path and the Buddhist perspective. Therefore, it is essential that anyone who embraces the Buddhist path study it and try to, first, understand it and, second, apply it.

Authentic Buddhist practice also requires an understanding of what liberation from samsara means. It is important to know the qualities of the state of nirvana and to generate a sincere aspiration to attain nirvana on the basis of this knowledge. Developing this aspiration occurs thanks to previously acquired knowledge of the characteristics and nature of samsara. This understanding allows us to generate authentic renunciation of samsara, which naturally leads to an aspiration to liberate ourselves from it.

These points are essential if we harbor a sincere wish to apply the Dharma. Without the aspiration to attain liberation and without renunciation of samsara, our practice of meditation is not fruitful. We can recite mantras, accomplish *yidam* practices, etc., but, in the absence of renunciation of samsara and aspiration toward liberation, our practice is not effective, and we do not obtain results. The Kagyü masters—as well as the Kadampas and those of Dzogchen—explain this point in particular.

The teachings on the four seals are thus essential in order to:
- Know the characteristics of samsara.
- Give rise to renunciation of samsara.
- Know the qualities of nirvana, or liberation.
- Develop the wish to attain liberation.

In general, everyone wishes to free themselves from samsara, and we often repeat, "I aspire to this ultimate felicity! I wish to actualize this state of supreme well-being. I want to attain liberation!"

However, we remain attached to samsara. We continue in an intermediate state; we wish for liberation, but we are still subject to our habitual functioning. We stagnate in a form of *bardo*,[13] incapable of moving forward in a given direction because we have not given rise to a sincere renunciation of samsara.

The aspiration for liberation in question here is not a casual wish such as, "Oh! How nice it would be if I could attain liberation!" It is a sincere wish that develops over the course of study and progressive understanding of the characteristics of this state. The process consists of:
- Studying the qualities of enlightenment;
- Acquiring absolute confidence in these qualities;
- Developing a conviction that obtaining this state

---

13 Intermediate state. In general, this term refers to the intermediate state between one life and the next.

means actualizing all of these qualities ourselves;
- Knowing the nature of this state.

Carrying out these steps gives rise to an unavoidable awareness within our minds: attaining liberation constitutes the sole option that allows us to put an end to suffering. There is no other solution.

Renunciation is essential for becoming aware of this necessity. Without it, liberation is not possible, as liberation specifically means giving up samsara definitively. Renunciation arises based on knowledge of the characteristics of samsara. We study them until we are convinced of them—in other words, until we have confirmed through our own experience that the nature of samsara is solely a source of suffering—an ocean of unhappiness.

When not a shadow of doubt remains in this regard, complete and authentic disillusionment takes place. It is no longer a vague remark such as, "It's true that things are kind of uncomfortable here," but an intimate realization that our present condition does not offer and will never offer us stable happiness and that samsara yields only unhappiness. Without disillusionment in regard to samsara and without aspiration for liberation, it is difficult to fully commit to Dharma practice and thus to gain the results of practice.

Knowledge of the characteristics and the nature of samsara gives rise to spontaneous and authentic renunciation. Based on this, we must then settle into regular meditation practice and persevere with this practice. In general—even if we sometimes meditate with great enthusiasm—we quickly tire of practice, while the success of meditation practice lies in its continuity and vigor.

A story rooted in one of the sutras that the master Shantideva retells in a stanza of the *Bodhicharyavatara*[14] illustrates this. This passage describes the conduct of the arhat Katyayana who lived during the time of Shakyamuni Buddha.

One day, a famous ruler invited this arhat to the palace. The king had carefully prepared a magnificent welcome ceremony to receive the arhat. He had stationed performers all along the boulevard leading up to the palace so that Katyayana was welcomed with song, dance, and a rain of flowers thrown across his path by a magnificent procession.

When he arrived at the palace, the king asked him, "Did you appreciate the welcome ceremony?"

Having attended to the most minute detail of the spectacle and décor, the king hoped for a positive response. The arhat replied, "I did not see anything on my way in. What ceremony are you speaking of?"

Very surprised, the king exclaimed, "How can it be that you did not see anything with all that we had organized?"

Facing the king's surprise and great disbelief, Katyayana insisted, "Truly, I did not see anything! I neither saw dancing nor heard music. The ceremony surely took place; I do not contest that, but—as for myself—I did not see it."

As the king continued to think it quite impossible that he had not seen anything, Katyayana asked him to bring a man who had been sentenced to death—the most dangerous criminal in the prison—to the palace and to

---

14 Shantideva, Batchelor, Stephen. *A Guide to the Bodhisattva's Way of Life [Bodhisattvacharyavatara].* Dharamsala: Library of Tibetan Works and Archives (LTWA), 1992-1993.

restage the ceremony for him. However, he added one condition. The criminal had to walk while holding a bowl filled to the brim with sesame seeds, and he could not drop a single seed. If the criminal failed to fulfill this condition, he would be executed on the spot by one of the four guards walking with him.

Thus, the criminal set out on his walk. Knowing that his life depended on it, he concentrated all of his attention on not dropping a single seed.

The ceremony was exactly the same as that performed for the arhat.

When the criminal arrived at the palace, Katyayana said to the king, "Ask him what he thought of the welcome ceremony."

The king obliged, and the criminal replied, "What ceremony? I did not see anything! What music and dance do you speak of?"

Now the king believed Katyayana and understood the teaching that the arhat was transmitting to him. When we focus on one thing, free from distraction, the sense faculties do not take in any other information. When we attain this level of concentration, the sense faculties no longer orient themselves on outer objects.

The goal is to develop the same level of concentration as Katyayana. Having meditated on suffering and on the unsatisfying aspects of samsara and having thus given rise to profound renunciation, his mind was completely and solely focused on liberation.

Therefore, training consists in keeping the mind focused on a single point, like the criminal whose life depended on it. Having seen the danger and being aware of it—in his case not that of samsara but of the four executioners ready to take his life upon the most minute error—he was fully focused on the task he had to accomplish in order to escape death.

When we are aware of the suffering of samsara, we train ourselves to maintain the same concentration as Katyayana or the criminal with no thought other than that of freeing ourselves. If we truly take the measure of samsara's suffering, and if we develop the aspiration toward liberation, we no longer experience attachment to outer objects. This is why the teaching emphasizes studying and understanding the characteristics and disadvantages of samsara. Strengthened by this understanding, authentic renunciation arises within us. Without this, meditation practice allows us to accumulate beneficial karma and merit, as it is a virtuous activity, but it is neither fruitful nor authentic—meaning that it does not lead to liberation.

There are various types of virtue, or beneficial karma, that we can accomplish and accumulate. Among them, there are three worth mentioning:
- The virtue that allows one to accumulate merit.
- The virtue that allows one to obtain liberation.
- The virtue that allows one to arrive at the path of seeing.

Let us look at these first two.

The virtue that allows one to accumulate merit refers to all beneficial actions that we carry out—free from any religious credo—such as acts of generosity or kindness that inspire us to help others.

These virtuous actions allow us to accumulate merit. As such, they constitute the causes for us meeting positive circumstances and experiencing well-being.

However, it is not certain that they constitute sufficient provisions for obtaining liberation. Thanks to all the virtuous actions we have accomplished in the past (which fall into this category of merit accumulation), we have obtained a precious human existence today. Furthermore, we likewise benefit from positive life conditions. We are in the West; we do not suffer from hunger or thirst. Even though we are currently experiencing an economic downturn, our basic living conditions remain acceptable. This is due to beneficial actions that we have accomplished in the past.

As we can observe, these acts were, nonetheless, not a sufficient cause for us to attain liberation. They simply allowed us to meet with positive conditions today.

Actions that fall into the category of Buddhist practice constitute *the virtue that allows one to obtain liberation.* Buddhist practitioners accomplish beneficial actions that lead them to liberation. When we practice with the goal of attaining liberation, we can say that our conduct is Buddhist.

Several questions may arise. What is the difference between Buddhist practice and non-Buddhist? Between virtuous actions that everyone carries out and those that are specifically Buddhist? Which practices lead to liberation?

Actions that are causes for merit accumulation cover all beneficial actions carried out with the goal of obtaining a certain happiness and good circumstances for oneself. This refers to everything we do while thinking of our own benefit in this life and future lives. A somewhat egocentric thought accompanies our action. "May these positive actions help me to obtain a good rebirth and positive circumstances in this life!"

Virtuous actions that are causes for obtaining liberation are based on knowledge of samsara's true nature, authentic renunciation, and the wish for liberation.

Understanding the difference between these two types of virtuous acts proves as vital as knowing what renunciation of samsara and the aspiration to become free from it mean. Without renunciation or the will to obtain liberation, the result of practice—be it mantra recitation, mandala offering, or meditation on a *yidam* or other deities—will be the same. If we carry out these virtuous activities appropriately, they constitute an accumulation of merit. If we do not carry them out appropriately, they can even contribute to accumulating negative karma!

A Buddhist must reflect on the following questions:
- What are the characteristics of samsara?
- What is samsara's true nature?
- How does renunciation come about?
- What are the characteristics of liberation?
- What are its qualities?
- How does one realize liberation?

Reflecting on these questions contributes to developing the necessary renunciation to progress along the path to liberation.

The four seals of the Dharma lead us to an understanding of the characteristics of samsara as well as the qualities and characteristics of liberation. This allows us to both renounce samsara and to aspire to liberation.

This teaching has two names: The Four Essences and The Four Seals. It is titled The Four Essences insofar as the four points sum up the essence of the Buddha's eighty-four thousand teachings of the Sutrayana and Tantrayana.

It is titled The Four Seals because the four points govern all phenomena of samsara and nirvana, just as a royal seal—once stamped on a document—commands the respect of all in the realm.

The four seals have their origin in the sutras and are as follows:

All conditioned phenomena are impermanent by nature.
All contaminated phenomena are suffering by nature.
All phenomena are empty and devoid of inherent existence.
Nirvana is a state of absolute peace.

The first two seals describe the characteristics of samsara:
- Samsaric phenomena are conditioned, and they are impermanent. This is their nature.
- They are nothing other than suffering because they are contaminated.

The last two seals designate the characteristics of nirvana or liberation.
- All phenomena are empty and devoid of inherent existence.
- Nirvana is a state of absolute peace.

I. All Conditioned Phenomena Are Impermanent by Nature.

The first seal that the Buddha taught is the fact that all conditioned phenomena are impermanent by nature.

The Reflection and Meditation on Impermanence

Reflection and meditation on impermanence are essential and offer countless inconceivable benefits.

In one of his works, Gampopa says:

The meditation on impermanence
Is very important in the beginning of practice,
It is very important during practice,
And it is very important at the end of practice.

The Importance of the Meditation on Impermanence in the Beginning of Practice

Without an awareness of our own impermanence,

we always put off Dharma practice for later, and we never fully commit to it, finding many reasons to put it aside. We apply ourselves to many worldly activities and, thus, lose precious time. We act this way because we believe ourselves to be eternal. In other words, we do not understand our own impermanence.

The meditation on impermanence occupies a central place in Dharma practice. Indeed, understanding that we are impermanent and that our current condition will not continue perpetually leads us to see the necessity of practicing the Dharma starting now.

Correct application of the Dharma requires gathering several positive conditions. Awareness of impermanence is the foundation for this.

The experience of contentment is another crucial factor. A person who is constantly dissatisfied gets easily carried away by the reigning desire of the moment. As such, the desire to acquire and accumulate more easily torments this type of person. If they possess something, they always want more or better. This state of mind reveals a lack of understanding of impermanence.

Meditating on impermanence leads to a satisfied and happy mind that does not get carried away by strong desires. Thus, the understanding of impermanence is a key factor for correctly beginning Dharma practice.

The Importance of the Meditation on Impermanence During Practice

This meditation also makes perseverance and consistency in our practice possible. It acts as a reminder of the transitory nature of life and of our present circumstances. We do not know how long our current situation will continue, and the moment of death can arrive instantly.

This awareness inspires us to think, "Now is the time to practice properly! Starting now, I must focus on creating beneficial causes, for at the moment of death, nothing else will be of any use to me; neither material possessions, nor all that I have accumulated in my lifetime, nor my friends. The Dharma and my provisions of positive karma will be the only truly useful things!"

Thanks to this state of mind, we understand the necessity of meditation practice, which naturally leads to greater perseverance—without which it is difficult to obtain liberation.

The following example is unpleasant, but it is a good reflection of our situation. We are like donkeys or other beasts of burden used in the past to labor fields. No animal carries out its task without being spurred on by the whip. Our behavior is rather similar. This meditation on impermanence plays the role of the whip that pushes us to practice correctly, as we do not do anything without this threat.

The meditation on impermanence is what leads to gaining awareness. It is difficult to undertake Dharma practice without motivation.

In one of his works, Gampopa shares the example of a deer enclosed in a cage. The animal is entirely dominated by the idea of getting out. If the cage opens, it flees in a sprint without a backward glance, as its greatest wish is to be free and never to be captive again.

Practitioners should act in the same way with their focus on liberation. They should feel the same anguish as the imprisoned deer and the same obsession with becoming free. This is how Milarepa lived and practiced. He applied himself solely to becoming free from samsara. He said to his disciple Rechungpa, "Do not ask me too many things because I hardly have the time!"

As soon as he encountered the Dharma—thanks to his awareness of the impermanence of his life and of all circumstances—he acted without wasting a minute in order to obtain liberation.

When meditation yields subtle awareness of impermanence, each instant becomes precious for practice to attain liberation. Even if we have not yet attained this high level of meditation, we can strive according to our ability for conduct that approaches it while working to attain this understanding.

The Importance of Meditation on Impermanence at the End of Practice

Gampopa explained that when we fully realize impermanence, we realize the *dharmakaya*[15]—the state of full enlightenment; Buddhahood—at the same time.

According to Gampopa, these two realizations—impermanence in all its subtlety and the dharmakaya—occur at the same time. Thus, this meditation is essential at the end of the path.

The meditation on impermanence is necessary in the beginning of practice because it allows us to start to apply the Dharma correctly. It is important all along the path in order to persevere and maintain our practice. And it is crucial at the end to obtain the result: enlightenment, or the realization of the dharmakaya.

In one of his sutras, Buddha Shakyamuni said,

---

15 "Awareness of the impermanence of all composite phenomena [...] becomes cause for the realization of the equal nature of all phenomena." in Gampopa, Ani K. Trinlay Chödron, Khenchen Könchog Gyaltshen Rinpoche. *The Jewel Ornament of Liberation: The Wish-fulfilling Gem of the Noble Teachings [dam chos rin po che yid bzhin nor bu thar pa rin po che'i rgyan/]*. New York: Snow Lion Publications, 1998, p. 91.

The meditation on impermanence brings about the
  same benefits
As every other Buddhist meditation,
And it brings together the essence of all Buddhist practices.
Meditating on impermanence with persistence
Is like making offerings to all the Buddhas.

Contemplating and realizing impermanence through meditation is essential to attain liberation. This idea is common to and explained in all Buddhist schools, whether they belong to the Theravada vehicle or Mahayana vehicle.

The story of a great meditator, the yogi called Kharak Gomchung, illustrates this theme. His name is known in the context of the teachings on mind training, as he belonged to the Kadam tradition that is at the origin of these instructions. Like Milarepa, his primary practice was that of impermanence. He lived as a recluse and meditated in a cave.

Each day, after his meditation, he left his cave and passed by a thorny shrub that blocked most of the entrance and tore his robe.

Then he thought, "I must cut back this plant."

Once outside, he said to himself, "What good is trimming the plant? I managed to get out, so it's not that important!"

On the way back in, he snagged his robe once more on the thorns and thought, "I must trim back this plant!"

Once he was inside again, he reflected, "I managed to get in once again, but who knows if I will go out again tomorrow, as death can come at any moment. I had better not waste any time, even a few minutes!"

Cutting the plant would have been short work, but the yogi had integrated the idea of impermanence to such a degree that a few minutes spent trimming the shrub seemed too great a loss of time to him. He nurtured this thought, "If I die tonight, what will have been the point? It is not really necessary."

The goal is to develop the same degree of awareness of impermanence. Then, worldly actions—even if they only take a few minutes—will seem like a waste of time to us.

As Shantideva said in the *Bodhicharyavatara*:

> *We do not know what will come first:*
> *Death or the next day.*

Meditating on impermanence allows us to become aware of the futility in planning for the future. In general, we devise many projects for the next year, for three years from now, etc. We prepare for what is ahead without having the slightest assurance that we will live long enough to carry out our plans, being as we are quite uncertain when the moment of our death will arrive. Life is unstable and no one can guarantee how much time we have left to live. Furthermore, there is no point in saying, "I am young. I have so much time ahead of me. That old person will surely die soon, for they are closer to death than I am."

Numerous examples show that this is far from the truth. Many people die while still young, and yet others continue life well into old age.

It is, likewise, pointless to say, "As I have no illnesses and am in very good health, I will probably live a long time, and those who are sick will likely die before me."

Nothing is guaranteed.

Even when circumstances are favorable and we are in good health, nothing is certain. Indeed, examples show that people in good health die before others who, despite a long illness, continue to live.

Life is unpredictable, and we remain quite unsure of how much time remains for us to live.

The causes of death are numerous and varied:

- Maturation of our karma.
- Exhaustion of merit or positive karma.
- Different types of obstacles.
- Exhaustion of our life force.

The following story illustrates the unpredictable nature of life:

One day, a wealthy man—strong and in good health—met a yogi who told him that he was going to die the following day.

At these words, the man thought, "How can it be that I will die tomorrow? To prevent every possible danger, I will not leave the house tomorrow."

He decided to stay home and relax without doing anything dangerous. He felt a need to clean one of his ears and got a Q-tip. While cleaning out his ear, he thought to himself, "How can it be that I am about to die? I am so young and in such good health."

A sudden noise rang out and made him jump. He stuck the Q-tip far into his ear and, in this way, he died.

Death is unpredictable. Some people die while eating; others in their sleep. They go to bed peacefully and do not wake up. We never know at what moment death will arrive. Therefore, meditation on impermanence is essential.

To find out if we are truly aware of impermanence, it is good to reflect regularly on the following question, "Am I truly aware of impermanence?"

The response will surely be, "Sometimes; occasionally."

The Two Forms of Impermanence

There are two forms of impermanence:

- Gross impermanence, which even animals perceive.
- Subtle impermanence.

Being aware of gross impermanence is insufficient for correct Dharma practice.

Gross Impermanence

This refers to basic awareness of mortal danger. Just like us, animals are endowed with this awareness of a fatal risk. Seeing other animals perish, they know that they too can die. If something pushes an animal toward a precipice, it refuses to jump. It senses that it is in danger and that it will die if it falls. Aware of the possibility of its death, it protects its life.

In general, each of us is aware of the possibility of death; either because we have already witnessed humans or animals dying or because we remember deceased people. For example, when we watch the news on television, we may learn that a great number of people have died at the same time in a plane crash or an earthquake.

This general awareness of death corresponds with what we call gross impermanence. We know that death exists and that people die.

Subtle Impermanence

The first of the four seals of the Dharma states that all conditioned phenomena are impermanent. Here, the Buddha refers to a subtler form of impermanence. It is worth developing this understanding of subtle impermanence because it serves as the antidote to mistaken thoughts and perspectives that we may have concerning our environment. These thoughts can push us to act in an improper way, and the actions we carry out based on this lack of understanding consequently generate situations of suffering and difficulty.

The primary mistaken view that leads us to act inappropriately (and, thus, to accumulate negative karma) is the belief that what we perceive is permanent and exists on its own, in a real and true way. To eliminate this inexact concept, it is essential that we acquire knowledge of subtle impermanence, as it is the only antidote that remedies this misunderstanding.

Subtle impermanence allows us to understand that all phenomena disappear, break down, or change because this is their nature. How does this happen? We can consider the example of a teacup. What makes a teacup impermanent?

It is necessary to arrive at a valid reason. For this, we need detailed explanations of subtle impermanence. This explanation has seven parts.

1. *Phenomena are impermanent because they are conditioned.*

The first reason that the Buddha gave in the sutras—and which we find elsewhere in various commentaries—is that a teacup is impermanent because it is a conditioned phenomenon.

The term *conditioned phenomena* refers to everything that appears on the basis of specific causes and conditions and whose existence depends on those same causes and conditions. If a phenomenon manifests on this basis, then it is impermanent.

A permanent phenomenon would not need outer causes and conditions other than itself to exist. It should exist on its own without depending on anything else. If it is permanent, a phenomenon should exist in the following manner:

- On its own.
- Without experiencing any change.
- Without depending on any external cause other than itself.

2. *Phenomena are impermanent because sometimes they exist and, at other times, they do not exist.*

If we continue the explanation with the example of the teacup, we can say that we currently perceive it and attribute an existence to it: the teacup is there. However, at some point, the teacup will break, and then it will no longer exist as a teacup.

A phenomenon that exists at certain moments then ceases to exist is, therefore, not a permanent phenomenon. A permanent phenomenon exists or does not exist, but if it is permanent, it must always remain the same.

If a phenomenon is endowed with the particularity of appearing according to certain circumstances and disappearing according to others, then it is an impermanent phenomenon because its appearance and disappearance depend on causes and conditions.

3. *Phenomena are impermanent because they change from moment to moment.*

If we continue with this example, another question arises. What makes the teacup impermanent? This is a fundamental question. Being capable of answering this question means that we have understood, or are capable of understanding, impermanence in all its aspects.

If I take a hammer and hit the teacup hard, it will break, and we can, then, say that what makes the teacup impermanent or what causes its destruction is the hammer or the hand that holds the hammer.

However, is this really what makes the teacup impermanent? Is the hammer truly the cause of its destruction? Are phenomena external to the teacup necessary for it to be impermanent?

The teacup is an example, but this reasoning applies to any outer phenomenon. The same is true for a grain of sand. Does the grain of sand require causes exterior to itself to disappear or is it impermanent by nature? If it is impermanent by nature, how is this so and why?

Let us return to the teacup. It is in our possession since the moment that we acquired it, but is yesterday's teacup the same as the teacup we perceive today?

If we had put a grain of sand on the table yesterday, and we looked at it today, would it be the same grain of sand or would it be different?

The teacup does not remain the same even for a single instant. It changes from moment to moment; therefore, it cannot be permanent.

4. *All phenomena are a series of instants.*
The teacup is part of a process of change that occurs instant after instant. Each one is different from the one

before it. This teacup that changes with each second is in an uninterrupted process of degeneration. A minute can be broken down into sixty seconds. Thus, there are sixty teacups, each different from the one before it. Phenomena are constantly changing in this way.

In general, we perceive phenomena to be unique and consistently identical to themselves. This is a mistaken idea. Due to this idea, we act in an inappropriate manner.

Thinking that this teacup is present today and will, likewise, be here tomorrow—but that if we break it, it will cease to exist—is an understanding of gross impermanence. This understanding is insufficient to act as an antidote that eliminates the misunderstanding that causes us to see phenomena as existing on their own in a concrete way. For this, the understanding of subtle impermanence—the fact that this teacup is in a process of change every moment—is essential.

Close to Vic runs a river called the Ter (it's a pretty name; in Tibetan, *ter* means treasure). Imagine we go to this river and have a drink. The following year, if we return to the waterway, we will naturally think that it is the same river and the same water. However, a few minutes' reflection is enough to realize that this is hardly the case. It is not the same water flowing because last year's water has already run out to the sea. The water currently making up the river is different water. All phenomena act identically to this river water; they change constantly. There is a form of continuity in this change. This continuum of moments resembles the uninterrupted movement of the river's water as it flows out to the sea.

This series of instants and changes is imperceptible to

us because we hold deeply to a persistent idea since beginningless time. According to us, things exist concretely and independently as phenomena that *are* truly present. These phenomena were here yesterday, are still present today, and remain identical from one moment to another.

We are not able to see their subtle changing because the idea of permanence is deeply rooted in our minds. Nevertheless, all phenomena are like a waterway: in constant movement; a continuum of moments of existence.

If the first instant of the teacup were permanent, there would be no second instant, and there would be no change. The change that occurs for the teacup—tarnishing and aging over time—would not occur. If the teacup were permanent—meaning that change did not exist—there would be no movement of instants.

Take our own case, for example. Our mothers give birth to us. In the beginning, we are newborns—cute and fragile—but the beings that we were have changed from moment to moment. Second after second, change occurs. Thanks to this, the process of growth was able to take place and we became the people that we are now who continue to change, to age, etc.

If the first instant were permanent, we would not change. A being would perpetually stay as it was.

As it is, all phenomena without exception go through three phases:

- A phase of birth, for living beings, or of creation, for objects.

- A phase of existence.

- A phase of death, destruction, or degeneration during which the phenomenon ceases to exist.

5. *Analysis of an Instant*

A question may then arise: are these three moments—birth, existence, and destruction—different or do they make up a single phase? Both options are correct. From a general point of view, it is correct to say that these three phases are different, but it is also relevant to suggest that they constitute a single phase. Affirming this idea is easy, but understanding it requires us to progress toward a deeper level. It is a question of a series of instants of change; therefore, we must understand that the first instant manifests, abides, and ceases before the second appears.

This can elicit new questions:

- Are the three phases of the first instant a single phase or can we divide them as well?

- Do all the phases occur in this first instant or does it only concern the manifestation phase? If so, the following phases—existence and cessation—do not occur.

- Does the first instant include these three phases?

- Do the three phases occur during the first instant?

Understanding this point is important. Gampopa underlines this when he writes in *The Jewel Ornament of Liberation*:

> *Awareness of the impermanence of all composite phenomena [...]*
> *becomes cause for the realization of the equal nature of*
> *all phenomena.*

This means that through understanding subtle impermanence, we simultaneously realize the *dharmakaya.*

Certain individuals hold that this first instant is *one*. Understanding this remains difficult.

All Buddhist scholars agree on the fact that this first instant appears and that the first phase is, therefore, present, but does this instant cease? Does it include the phase of cessation?

For example: I have been born, but am I dead? Birth and death: are they identical or are they different?

The first moment—that of appearance—is *I am born*. But am I dead also?

Let us take a closer look at these questions.
- What does it mean *to be born*?
   This means *to exist*.
- What does it mean *to die*?
   This means *to no longer exist*.

As we can see, these two states are distinctly different. We already mentioned that this first instant is made up of a phase of manifestation—and, thus, existence—and that being dead corresponds with no longer existing. Can this instant then be simultaneously existent and non-existent? Can these two aspects be present simultaneously in a single instant?

The sutras, but also all of the scholars of the past—both Indian and Tibetan—agree that this first instant manifests and also ceases.

If it did not cease, this conclusion would be incoherent and is not logical. Nothing external to the instant itself causes its end. Nothing and no one make it cease; it does so itself. It is the nature of the instant itself to manifest and to disappear.

In the example of the teacup, we saw that if it fell from the table or if we hit it with a rock, it would break. In this case, we may think that the cause of the teacup breaking is the fall or the rock. However, we cannot apply this same reasoning to the cessation of an instant, for we clearly see that it does not depend on an external factor. As such, it is indeed because this instant appeared that it then ceases. Such is its very nature: to appear and to cease. Nothing external intervenes in this process. One aspect brings about the other.

Thinking that an external factor is responsible for the appearance and cessation of phenomena hinders us from understanding subtle impermanence.

The three phases of appearance, existence, and cessation occur within a single instant and do not constitute three distinct phases from one another.

6. *The Interdependence of Appearance and Cessation*

We may think that the moment of cessation of the instant only depends upon itself and not on anything else, as it does not depend on external circumstances. This is not the case either because the cessation of an instant depends on its appearance—in other words, on the event from which it arose. Appearance and cessation depend on one another. Thus, we cannot say that the cessation of this instant is a completely independent phenomenon, but rather that it depends on its appearance or its production. It ceases *because* it has appeared.

This is what subtle impermanence refers to. Trying to understand this point is essential.

7. *The Importance of the Reflection on Impermanence*

As we have seen, all conditioned phenomena are impermanent. The expression *conditioned phenomena* refers to all phenomena—both outer, such as material objects, mountains, and places, and inner, like beings. In samsara, there are not conditioned phenomena that are impermanent and others that are permanent. Everything that depends on causes and conditions—therefore, all of samsara's phenomena—is impermanent by nature.

Each of these phenomena can be compared to a bubble, a ray of light, a cloud, or a dream in that they are ephemeral and transitory.

Even those that seem the most lasting or permanent to us—like mountains that seem to remain identical for millennia and certainly much longer than we do—are also subject to change and impermanence. From moment to moment, change occurs within matter. Like a fish constantly moving in the water—never staying still—all phenomena are in constant movement.

In general, gross impermanence is easy to approach and understandable thanks to the observation that objects are not lasting and, as such, they eventually cease to exist. As for subtle impermanence, it consists in understanding that change occurs in every moment. Even us—we are not identical to what we were yesterday—and objects are not the same as they were an hour ago. Change occurs every second. Succeeding in recognizing the two levels of impermanence in all phenomena that we perceive is essential.

Listening to a sound allows us to observe that it ceases after several seconds. This is a manifestation of impermanence. We may also notice that what we think about changes constantly and, thus, is likewise impermanent. It is not so much a question of perceiving impermanence in all that surrounds us, but, rather, of recognizing it.

Two examples illustrate this theme. The first concerns Milarepa, the great yogi who spent all of his life in solitary locations dedicating his time to meditation. He had nothing to eat or drink and, as it were, no clothes to wear. His sole possession was an earthenware pot in which he occasionally cooked nettles gathered in the mountains. One day, he decided to move to a new cave, taking with him the pot that was his only belonging. As the mountain paths were quite steep, he slipped and fell, and his pot broke. At the moment that it shattered, he sang this *vajra* song:

> *All conditioned phenomena are impermanent;*
> *Precious human rebirth is also impermanent;*
> *My pot is broken; thank you!*

At that very moment, Milarepa considered his pot to be his master or lama, for this event allowed him to see with great clarity that all phenomena are impermanent and that the pot was not so important. He felt true gratitude toward the situation and the loss of his cookware.

Indeed, we hear a great many teachings on impermanence, but once we leave the teaching hall, we become distracted and do not pay attention to what surrounds us. We do not recognize impermanence within our own environment, although only a little vigilance would make us aware of its presence in all aspects of our lives. We should react like Milarepa!

The second story is that of a meditator who had a friend called Spirit. One day, this meditator felt his strength declining.

He called Spirit to him and said, "As you have the

ability to know the exact moment of death, please warn me when this moment is approaching for me."

His friend gave his word and told the meditator not to worry and that he would inform him or give him a sign.

Some time later, Spirit returned and told him, "Today, up on the mountain, someone died."

Another day, he came to visit and said, "Today, in the valley, someone died."

He came to see him again and said, "Today, one of our neighbors died."

Several days later, the meditator fell gravely ill and realized that his end was near. Very upset that his friend had not warned him, he reprimanded Spirit, "You promised to give me some indication that I would soon die. Why didn't you do so?"

"I warned you three times," replied Spirit. "I tried to inform you, but you never paid attention to my warnings."

This is what happens to all of us. Indeed, every day when we watch the news or read the newspaper, we see that many people have lost their lives. However, we do not pay attention. We continue on our road without preparing for death. Not only do we not prepare for it, but we act as though we will live forever. Occasionally, we think, "One day I will die, but that is of no importance to me!"

The moment of death is a difficult trial we will have to face. The process of the elements' dissolution can be very harrowing. Preparing ourselves allows us to navigate death without burden or fear.

In general, we are not very attentive to objects' or people's impermanence—even that of those close to us who pass away. We have a difficult time feeling concerned about our own impermanence. Nevertheless, when the moment of death arrives, we will start to tremble in fear, but it will be too late to prepare ourselves. Furthermore, if we have committed negative acts in the past, we will feel deep regret. However, we will no longer have the time to repair or find solutions to the misdeeds we have committed—nor to purify them in one way or another. It will be too late. This sensation of worry, fear, anger or attachment to life will continue in the bardo after death and will give rise to the manifestation of terrifying experiences.

We are like a traveler staying in a hotel. Our consciousness is the traveler and the body we have in this life is the hotel. A moment will come when he will have to leave, but the traveler cannot take the hotel with him even if he likes it very much. In the same way, our consciousness must one day leave this body and can neither take the body with itself in the process of death, nor into the following life. Consciousness must leave the body behind.

This body constitutes our most prized possession. Life is what counts the most for us—what we cherish the most dearly. All the same, we will have to abandon it when the moment of death comes.

When we ask ourselves, "Who is the true owner of my life?" we generally answer, "I am the owner of my life."

In reality, the owner of our lives is the lord of death or, more precisely, impermanence. We can stay in a hotel so long as we are able to pay the bill, but when we run out of money or when the owner decides it is time for us to go, we have to leave the premises. We do not know exactly how much time remains to us in this place. This is the same for both body and mind. The traveler (our consciousness) must understand that they will have to leave one day. Therefore, they would do well to prepare themself, to take care of their affairs, and seek out a place where they can go next.

In general, we do not prepare ourselves and, when death suddenly arrives, we do not know where to go or what to do. Preparing ourselves is essential.

As Nagarjuna said:

> *Our lives are as fragile as a candle flame*
> *Placed on a windy day*
> *In a room with an open window.*

We do not know precisely at what moment the wind will blow out the candle, just as we do not know when the moment of our death will be. The conditions that can bring it about are innumerable, and we can die at any moment. Becoming aware of this allows us to understand that a single day of life is a like a gift that we must appreciate and use properly because it is precious.

In the text entitled *Letter to a Friend*[16], Nagarjuna says:

> *With all its many risks, this life endures*
> *No more than windblown bubbles in a stream*
> *How marvelous to breathe in and out again,*
> *To fall asleep and then awake refreshed.*

---

16 Kyabje Kangyur Rinpoche, Nagarjuna, Padmakara Translation Group. *Nagarjuna's Letter to a Friend [Suhṛllekha].* Ithaca: Snow Lion Publications, 2005, p. 49.

This is the real miracle and not all the other kinds of things that we consider amazing.

The theme of impermanence is quite vast. If you wish to delve deeper into the subject, you can refer to Gampopa's text *The Jewel Ornament of Liberation*.

It explains gross impermanence with examples such as the rotation of day and night, of the sun and moon, or of the changing seasons. We can observe that flowers blossom in the spring, fruit ripen in autumn, and plants die in winter. These examples are manifest expressions of impermanence. Gampopa also discusses subtler impermanence, but in a less detailed manner. The explanations given here come from certain sutras and commentaries.

When we undertake a spiritual path like the Buddhist path, understanding and being aware of impermanence (that of all that surrounds us as well as our own) is a necessary element of our practice. Therefore, it is necessary to:

- Meditate on our own impermanence and our own death.

- Reflect on the fact that death is inevitable.

- Consider that we do not know when the moment of death will come because it is unpredictable.

- Contemplate the innumerable circumstances that lead to death, which are considerably more numerous than those that preserve life.

- Meditate on the various points regarding subtle impermanence and also on the fact that a process of change occurs from moment to moment.

If we pursue our reflection on impermanence, we realize that the most powerful people in history—who possessed great authority and fabulous wealth—could not escape death. Today, nothing remains of them other than their biographies.

Highly accomplished beings such as the arhats or the Buddha himself also experienced the process of death when the moment came. Therefore, it is evident that we will not escape. We are like soap bubbles blown by the wind. Death can overtake us at any moment. This is why the meditation on impermanence remains at the heart of Buddhist practice.

By meditating on impermanence, we develop a certain contentment. We develop less attachment to our possessions and do not wish to acquire so many things.

Becoming truly aware of impermanence and understanding that it is the nature of all conditioned phenomena—of both samsara and nirvana—as the Buddha said, is a key point of the path for Buddhist practitioners in particular.

The Buddha said, "All conditioned phenomena are impermanent."

He did not say, "Some are permanent, and others are impermanent."

Meditating on impermanence leads us to realize the value of time and gives rise to a need within us to practice the Dharma. Thanks to this new awareness, we wish to make the most of the time we have because we now know that impermanence is cutting it down at every moment.

This reasoning is familiar. In general, we think that we have a given amount of time and that we will dedicate a certain period to one thing and another period to another thing, but this is not in accordance with reality.

Impermanence has already begun to eat away at the time we have, and so we should accord our time its true value and devote it to meaningful activities. Meditating on impermanence allows us to make the most of each minute we have.

Yesterday belongs to the past. Whatever we did then—be it harmful or beneficial, useful or not—yesterday is gone. No one, however powerful they may be, can say, "I am going to take yesterday's time for today, I will keep today's for tomorrow." Using the present moment wisely is essential. Meditation on impermanence leads us specifically to realize the value our time has so that we can put it to good use and not waste it.

We can compare our lives to the sun. We see it rise in the east in the morning, but soon evening comes, and the sun disappears in the west. Since our birth, each passing moment brings us closer to our death, and nothing can stop this movement. We are now closer to death than to birth. Even if we do not wish to die, death will come for us. This is the lot of all living beings. No animal, no insect—even the most minute—wishes to die. All beings wish to live as long as possible, but we all eventually face death. Nothing and no one can stop this inexorable process of impermanence that brings us ever closer to death.

It is possible to stop the clock and say, "I would like twelve o'clock to go on for several hours," but even if the clock is frozen, time itself goes on. Even if we could harness the sun and hold it back so that night never fell and rejoice in the feeling that time had ceased to pass, we could not fool ourselves. Time would continue to pass, and, at some point, a moment would come that we would be tired and would need to sleep.

The story of the Indian *mahasiddha* Virupa illustrates this point. In India, it can be very hot. The temperature can go up to 113° Fahrenheit (45° Celsius). One day during a heat wave, Virupa felt quite thirsty, went into a tavern, and ordered the bartender to serve him a beer. The bartender was no fool and knew that this type of "mad" yogi often left without paying.

She did not bring him a drink and instead told him, "Pay me first. If you do not pay me, I will not serve your beer."

The yogi replied, "Don't worry. I assure you that I will pay."

She responded, "No. First, you pay, and after, I will give you the beer."

In truth, Virupa did not have any money to pay for his drink. He stuck a stick in the earth and drew a line in front of its shadow. Then, he said to the tavern owner, "When the stick's shadow crosses the line on the ground, I will pay you immediately."

She agreed and served him a beer.

Virupa began to drink his beer. Then, he drank a second. And another and another until he had cleaned out the tavern's supply. The shadow had yet to pass the line on the ground.

Still, the owner said to him, "Now you have to pay me!"

"No," he said, "we had an agreement."

"But I don't have any more beer," she cried.

"That is not my problem. We made a deal according to which you give me beer so long as the shadow has not crossed this line. You must try to find more beer in some other taverns because you gave me your word."

The story goes that he drank all of the available beer from five hundred different establishments without the sun ever changing its location. The inhabitants of the country and its ruler were surprised and did not understand what was happening. The sun shone without pause. The day continued endlessly, and the people kept working without any rest. As it was still bright out, everyone continued with their labors. However, the fatigue began to set in, and the workers began to make mistakes.

Seeing this, the king wondered, "What can we do to fix this situation?"

He gathered together his advisors in order to find a solution. His advisors did not have any more ideas than the king. Therefore, the king sent his advisors to investigate the cause of this occurrence. However, finding useful information proved a challenge.

The tavern owner witnessed the king's advisors going about their investigation. She went to see them and explained, "It is likely that the yogi in my tavern is responsible for what is happening."

Several days had gone by, but the sun had not budged at all. The yogi held it in place, preventing its progress across the sky with a *mudra.*

The king addressed the yogi, "Is it you who holds back the sun?"

He replied, "Yes."

The king ordered him to free the sun, but the yogi replied, "I cannot."

"Why?" inquired the king.

"If I let the sun go, I have to pay for all the beer I drank, and I do not have any money. And so, I cannot free the sun."

Therefore, the king replied, "I will pay your drink.

Please, free the sun!"
The yogi then told him that he owed money not only at this tavern, but in five hundred others as well, and he had to pay them all. When the king had agreed to cover all of his debts, then Virupa let the sun go.

This story shows that everything is impermanent, and even if we want to stop time by stopping the clock, it will continue to pass because that is the nature of all things. Everything is impermanent.

The masters of the Kagyü and Kadam lineages emphasize this in their oral instructions, and various Dzogchen teachings focus on this point as well. The goal is to become familiar with impermanence—to study it and meditate on it so that we can fully integrate the notion and, in this way, use our lives for practice.

This meditation must include all that surrounds us: our being and our own life as well as subtle impermanence.

When we manage to reflect and meditate on subtle impermanence through to its full integration, then we realize emptiness and the *dharmakaya.*

That is the essential meaning of this first seal, which emphasizes that conditioned phenomena are impermanent.

Q&A

Question: The relationship between two instants is not a causal relationship, then, but simply the fact that the cessation of one brings about the appearance of the other?

Answer: No, there is indeed a causal relationship between the first and the second instant because the second instant is the result of the first instant or because the first instant is the cause of the second.

In terms of the first instant, the three phases of appearance, existence, and cessation occur. We tried to determine if these three moments make up a single phase or whether they are three distinct phases. This was the subject of our reflection.

According to Mahayana Buddhism, the conclusion is that these three phases occur within a single instant. Therefore, they represent the very essence or nature of the instant.

It is important to understand this in the context of meditation practice, for the nature of this instant is to appear, remain, and cease. These occurrences are not three separate instances.

Here, I offer a simple explanation of this point, but to arrive at an unshakeable certainty and in order to be able to experience this for oneself, much more thorough analysis, reflection, and meditation—employing a technique called analytical meditation—are necessary. This meditation consists in intimately examining and reflecting upon a subject until we reach absolute certainty based on understanding and personal experience.

II. All Contaminated Phenomena Are Suffering by Nature

In this context, *contaminated phenomena* refers to afflicted states of mind: afflictive emotions.

In samsara, all phenomena that appear on the basis of our afflictive emotions and karma are contaminated by these emotions and by karma. This is why all contaminated phenomena are suffering by nature.

The Different Types of Suffering

The theme of suffering is vast, for it includes many forms.

The Suffering of Birth, Sickness, Old Age, and Death

All beings experience the four types of suffering of birth, sickness, old age, and death. These types of suffering are specific to living beings. For example, external objects do not experience them.

The Suffering of Experiencing What We Do Not Wish For

Another form of suffering that living beings face is experiencing things that we do not wish for. For example, no one wishes to have enemies or to get hurt. Nevertheless, we have to deal with these types of situations.

We do not wish to suffer from hunger or thirst, but we often experience this type of suffering. We have no desire to be separated from our loved ones, and yet we must face this hardship at one point or another.

Whatever our initial desires may be, we nevertheless have to face situations that we do not wish for, which causes unhappiness.

Societal problems, such as economic crises, are situations that we do not want to experience, yet, all the same, we are subject to them. Environmental problems like climate change or earthquakes are, likewise, types of suffering that no one wishes to deal with and yet we must face them also. The same is true for personal problems in daily life.

No one wants to get sick, and yet it is very difficult to avoid. When we do fall ill, we have to face the experience of being sick and also to take various unpleasant medicines with uncomfortable side effects. Even if we are not happy about this, we have no choice. It may happen that we require surgery, which is never pleasant, but we have to accept it all the same.

This inevitable confrontation with numerous situations that we do not wish for generates suffering—both physical and mental (and there are infinitely more types of mental suffering)—that we have no choice but to face as living beings.

The Suffering of Being Unable to Obtain What We Desire

The opposite of the previous form of suffering is that of being unable to obtain what we desire. This is, likewise, a source of dissatisfaction.

In general, we desire many things: happiness, good luck, wealth, good friends, and an easy life, but these very often escape us.

Desire alone is insufficient to acquire what we wish for. We must invest a lot of effort to get what we want. Furthermore, these efforts are not always effective or a measure of success. This, then, is another form of samsara's suffering—precisely because samsara's nature is suffering.

We also want the best for our parents, our children, and our friends. We want them to be happy. However, no matter how hard we may wish, they nevertheless encounter difficulties, get sick, or face other hardships.

It is difficult to make an exhaustive list of all the different types of suffering living beings experience because they are as numerous as the beings that inhabit samsara.

In general, we can speak of four principal types of suffering that human beings experience:
- Birth
- Sickness
- Old Age
- Death

To this, we can add the suffering of experiencing what we do not wish for and the suffering of being unable to obtain what we desire.

However, there are many more types of suffering, as beings face infinite forms of hardship in samsara.

Guru Rinpoche expressed it in this way:

It is said that in this samsara there is not as much
As a pinpoint's worth of happiness to be found.
But should one happen to find just a little,
It will contain the suffering of change.[17]

We cannot find the smallest amount of happiness in samsara, not even so much as would fit on a pinpoint.

Maitreya also expressed this fact with the following couplet:

Just as there are no good smells in a cesspit,
There is no happiness among the five classes of beings.[18] [19]

Just like a toilet, samsara reeks. Whatever destination we reach in rebirth, we will experience suffering. At times, we may have the impression of being happy, but this happiness never lasts.

The Three Basic Forms of Suffering

We can distinguish three basic forms of suffering:
- The Suffering of Suffering
- The Suffering of Change
- Existential Suffering

These three forms of suffering are the nature of all samsaric phenomena.

---

17 Patrul Rinpoche, previously cited Footnote 3, p.137.

18 We count five states of existence (instead of six) when not distinguishing the demi-gods from the gods.

19 Patrul Rinpoche, previously cited Footnote 3, p.137.

The Suffering of Suffering

This type of suffering is the most obvious. It refers to the unpleasant presence of suffering when it manifests. So long as it is present, we experience unhappiness. When this type of suffering ceases, we experience well-being. The sutras define it in this way. A question may arise: how does it manifest?

If we experience mental suffering and, in addition, we must endure physical illness, then we can speak of physical suffering. Furthermore, if our friends are also facing difficulties and this causes us even greater unhappiness, we can speak of accumulated suffering. This type of suffering refers to those moments when we recognize a situation as suffering. Even animals experience this type of suffering.

The Suffering of Change

This type of suffering is equivalent to what we call "temporary well-being in samsara."

When a feeling of well-being arises, we perceive it for as long as it lasts, but when it goes away or when it changes, a form of suffering appears: the suffering of change. For example, imagine we go on a picnic in the countryside on a beautiful day. We bring everything we need, and we settle down in a lovely spot. Then, suddenly, a storm breaks out, transforming the initial situation. The unhappiness caused by change is a form of suffering.

This example focuses on an insignificant problem, but certain situations are much more serious. A delicious meal that later causes us to be sick also constitutes suffering due to a change in the initial situation. Animals, likewise, experience this form of unhappiness.

This type of suffering affects us more acutely when

we have a high degree of attachment to things, circumstances, or people. The suffering is then infinitely greater, as when we lose someone dear to us. When there is less attachment, we suffer less.

The following story illustrates this point:

In a charming field of flowers, there lived a colony of bees. On a fine sunny day, one of the youngest bees decided to go out and enjoy the beautiful location and the cool breeze that was blowing. She flew to where the best flowers were blooming and set about gathering pollen. Then, an idea came to her, "I should come back here with all of my friends and family so they can enjoy it, too."

She consumed the flower's pollen all while thinking how delicious it was. Then, she moved on to another flower that she found to be even more splendid. She carried on in this way, all the while imagining the next day's happiness when she would return with her family and friends to this delightful place.

In the evening, she landed on a flower. As night was falling, the flower closed, imprisoning the bee inside. Then she thought, "What shall I do now? How can I get out of here?"

She calmed herself and reflected, "There is no problem. I have a lot of pollen to enjoy. I am going to have a good meal, and tomorrow I will go get my friends and family so that we can enjoy this place together."

Suddenly, in the midst of eating her pollen, she heard a thundering noise—a great crashing coming closer and closer. It was an elephant out for a walk. He was headed in her direction. As he passed by, he crushed the bee inside the flower.

This is yet another example of the suffering of change. While the situation of well-being lasts, we believe ourselves to be happy, but as soon as the situation changes, the initial happiness gives way to suffering, especially if we are very attached to what we desire. Without some measure of contentment in our minds, the suffering of change will affect us greatly. The bee found herself in a similar situation. She was happy and believed that all was well despite things not going as she had planned. Then, as soon as she heard the crashing sound of the elephant's footsteps, the situation changed, and she began to feel terror and great suffering, which continued up to the moment of her death.

Animals are conscious of the first two types of suffering and try to avoid them. It is important that we—human beings endowed with greater intelligence—try to integrate them in our reflection and practice.

Awareness of current suffering in samsara causes disillusionment. However, which form of suffering is the basis for renunciation of samsara? Is it the suffering of suffering, the suffering of change, or existential suffering?

Renunciation of samsara and the suffering it includes does not refer to the suffering of suffering nor to the suffering of change, for even animals wish to be free from these. Renunciation consists in understanding that everything in samsara is suffering. This understanding arises thanks to the explanation of the third type of suffering: existential suffering.

Existential Suffering

Being born in samsara means experiencing suffering. Existential suffering includes everything; there is no place we can go to escape it because it pervades everything at every moment. However, recognizing it and perceiving it remain difficult.

One of the sutras explains that if we place a hair in the palm of our hand and we close our eyes, we do not feel it. The same is true for existential suffering; it is present, but we do not perceive it. By contrast, if we put this same hair in our eye, it will bother us greatly and even cause us pain. We will do everything we can to remove it as quickly as possible.

Noble beings who see reality for what it is perceive the existential suffering that accompanies all rebirth in samsara this way.

Renunciation of samsara's suffering refers to renunciation of existential suffering.

In Tibetan, the adjective that describes this type of suffering is *kyapa pa*, which means *all-pervasive*, signifying that this suffering is omnipresent in samsara. This suffering exists everywhere, in every moment. It arises anew with each moment. It pervades all contaminated phenomena—be they outer phenomena such as objects or inner phenomena such as beings.

Being born means being endowed with the five aggregates:
- The Aggregate of Forms or Physical Aggregates
- The Aggregate of Sensations
- The Aggregate of Distinctions
- The Aggregate of Formations
- The Aggregate of Consciousness

We refer to these aggregates as "contaminated" because they are the result of karma and afflictive emotions. They are, by nature, marked by the seal of suffering, which causes us, in turn, to experience suffering. From the first moment of our lives in conjunction with these contaminated aggregates, we experience change due to the impermanence of all samsaric phenomena. From moment to moment, we change.

Subtle impermanence makes up existential suffering. From our first moment, we embark on an inevitable process of aging that generates this existential suffering—so called because it touches all of samsaric existence. Like space, which surrounds the entire world and is everywhere, this omnipresent suffering pervades all phenomena within samsara.

We seek precisely what evades us: stable happiness that does not change; ultimate joy free from transformation. Whatever situation of well-being we may find ourselves in, it is destined to change due to impermanence. Everything changes from moment to moment. No well-being, no sensation, no experience of happiness, can last due to this impermanence. This is what constitutes omnipresent suffering. On the basis of this understanding, renunciation arises and we attain liberation in the end.

The experience of all other suffering occurs on the basis of existential suffering. It is the sole root. The instability of everything that surrounds us and of our relationships generates the suffering we experience in daily life. This suffering is inherent in impermanence. Sometimes, we have friends and believe in their kindness, but suddenly, they become enemies. Other times, we think we can trust certain people, but we are disappointed.

Nothing is stable in samsara. Our own experience confirms it. On a subtler level, this instability refers to the suffering inherent in existence.

In a stanza from the Bodhicharyavatara,[20] Shantideva says:

One moment they are friends,
And in the next instant they become enemies.
Since they become angry even in joyful situations,
It is difficult to please ordinary people.

Samsara's instability generates countless different types of suffering. We can observe this in our own lives. Furthermore, if we extrapolate and consider future lives, we can observe even stranger situations. Through this process, friends and loved ones in this life can become enemies in the following existence. The opposite is also true. People who were our enemies can appear as our best friends in a subsequent life. As a result, this suffering makes no sense.

There is an anecdote to illustrate this theme:

One day, Katyayana went out with his alms bowl to beg for food. Coming upon a house, he saw a man holding an infant in his lap. The man was eating a fish and throwing stones to keep a dog away because she was munching on the fish bones. Owing to his clairvoyance, the arhat was able to perceive the scene from the perspective of this life as well as past lives. He recited this verse:

He eats his father's flesh, he beats his mother off,
He dandles on his lap the enemy that he killed;
The wife is gnawing at the husband's bones.
I laugh to see what happens in samsara's show![21]

---

20 Shantideva, Batchelor, Stephen. *A Guide to the Bodhisattva's Way of Life [Bodhisattvacharyavatara]*. Dharamsala: Library of Tibetan Works and Archives (LTWA), 1992-1993, p. 103.

21 Patrul Rinpoche, previously cited Footnote 3, p.51.

He saw clearly that the fish had been the man's father, the dog had been his mother, and the infant, his enemy in another life.

In samsara, everything is unstable in this way, and, as a result, we must experience a great deal of senseless suffering.

The Suffering of the Six Realms of Samsara

The theme of suffering is vast, as are the aspects we can cover in this subject. An examination of the six realms of samsara allows us to get a general idea.

The Hell Realms

The primary forms of suffering in the hell realms are those of extreme heat and cold. There are eighteen different hell realms:

- Eight Hot Hells
- Eight Cold Hells
- The Neighboring Hells
- The Ephemeral Hells

The suffering related to the hot and cold temperatures the beings in the conditions of the hot and cold hells experience is unimaginable. It is impossible for human beings to envision such intense suffering. Furthermore, the lifespans within these realms are so long that we cannot count them in years.

Many texts cover the theme of hellish existences. We will not go into a detailed description here. Studying the suffering that occurs in these states profoundly affects us and inspires us to act immediately to avoid rebirth in these conditions.

It is beyond our abilities to perceive this suffering, so it is easy to ignore it and let it slip from our minds. The

Buddha gave teachings on these realms several times, as we see in the sutras, and several masters capable of perceiving hellish existences described them as well.

The term *ephemeral hells* refers to the suffering that insects and other beings born within excrement or cesspools experience.

From among the many stories illustrating this type of fate, here is one from the 9th Karmapa.

One day, when the 9th Karmapa Wangchuk Dorje was a child, he was out for a walk. Suddenly, he stopped before a great boulder. He drew closer to it and began to beat it with his garment until the stone opened up. When the two halves of the rock fell away, he could see a very ugly insect within. Karmapa immediately made wishes to save the insect and to allow it to obtain a better rebirth. In this way, the insect was later reborn in more favorable conditions.

This type of rebirth is considered to be rebirth in the ephemeral hells (*nitsewa* in Tibetan). The insect was living within the rock without food or drink, having been born there as a result of its karma. It had no choice but to accept the suffering that its life included. These forms of suffering refer to the seventeenth hell realm.

The Hungry Ghost Realm (*yidak* in Tibetan or *preta* in Sanskrit)

These beings' karma leads them to primarily experience suffering related to extreme hunger and thirst.

Certain beings of this kind may sometimes perceive a river due to positive karmic imprints. However, when they approach it, the river dries up or disappears. Finding food proves very difficult, and even more so finding good food. Furthermore, on the rare occasions when these beings manage to acquire pus or blood for a meal, they are not even able to consume it because it transforms into fire when they bring it to their mouths. Such are their life conditions for innumerable years during which they experience only suffering!

The force of karma is very complex, as the following story illustrates.

During the time of Buddha Shakyamuni, one of his most devoted disciples, Ananda, went out for a walk one evening. On his way, he encountered a preta who had just given birth to five hundred preta newborns. She had an enormous stomach and a miniscule mouth. She begged him for something to eat. Ananda had nothing to offer her. The preta then predicted that he had only seven days to live and would die after one week.

Ananda, panicking at the idea of his subsequent death, went to see the Buddha, recounted his encounter, and begged him for a way to extend his life. The Buddha replied that there was no need to worry, as there are various meditation practices that can remedy such situations.

These practices consist in reciting various *sadhanas*[22] that allow the practitioner to develop generosity for this type of being by means of specific prayers and mantras. Due to the power of these mantras, the pretas are able to find food and satisfy their hunger. Ananda carried out all of these practices, which allowed him to free himself from his current obstacles and to extend his life.

One of the sutras explains that acts of generosity dedicated to this type of being are the most powerful. Indeed, the sutra explains that acts of generosity fo-

---

22 Meditation practice texts from the Tantric path.

cused on helping or protecting beings experiencing great suffering or deprivation allow us to accumulate immense merit.

The Animal Realm

Animals, likewise, experience innumerable forms of suffering. Among them, the most notable are ignorance and lack of freedom. Animals often find themselves under human domination. Human masters force them to work and obey without the possibility of release from the yoke.

The Human Realm

As we previously discussed, human beings face four types of suffering—birth, sickness, old age, and death— in addition to constant worry and the inability to attain what they desire.

The Demigod Realm (Realm of the *asuras* in Sanskrit)

These beings endure the suffering of constant conflict with the gods.

The Divine Realm or the Realm of Celestial Beings

Beings in this realm see their death and subsequent place of rebirth in samsara before it arrives, which causes them intolerable suffering.

The different forms of suffering described here explain the most basic themes, but it is possible to say much more on the subject. This explanation is merely a summary of all the suffering that beings may encounter in samsara. You can find all the details in the sutras, in Gampopa's book *The Jewel Ornament of Liberation*, and in Patrul Rinpoche's text, *The Words of My Perfect Teach-*

er. Vasubandhu's work *The Abhiharmakosha*[23] describes the various realms of samsara in the most minute detail.

The Importance of the Reflection on Liberation from Suffering

Aspiration toward liberation is an essential factor for correct and authentic Dharma practice. However, the goal is not merely to obtain happiness and well-being in this life solely for oneself. Through attentive analysis of the dissatisfying characteristics and aspects of samsara, we reach this certainty: this condition is pure suffering. A form of renunciation arises based on this conviction. Disillusionment regarding samsara is the basis for the wish to attain liberation. The criteria that define an authentic practitioner are authentic renunciation and sincere aspiration for liberation based on the four seals of the Dharma.

The Buddhist method includes a unique characteristic that distinguishes it from other religious or philosophical schools: its perspective on reality. Correctly understanding this perspective is essential because it is the correct and appropriate view for an individual who wishes to commit to the path of enlightenment. The purity of the path depends on the purity of the view that we adopt. If our view is erroneous, then we will not undertake the appropriate path—the path that leads to enlightenment. The Buddhist view is both vast and profound. Understanding it and following it makes us Buddhist practitioners. In addition, we must practice with the motivation to attain liberation.

---

23 To read this work and its commentary in English, see: Choephel, David Karma, Ninth Karmapa, Wangchuk Dorje, Vasubandhu. *Jewels from the Treasury: Vasubhandu's Verses on the Treasury of Abhidharma And Its Commentary Youthful Play.* Woodstock: KTD Publications, 2012.

As we have discussed previously, there are several types of virtuous action. Some contribute only to the accumulation of merit, while others are causes for obtaining liberation. A Buddhist practitioner specifically accomplishes beneficial practices focused on realizing liberation. To be considered part of this category, the key point is to develop certainty that remaining in samsara is suffering. It is not a question of believing in this statement, but rather a matter of reflecting until we give rise to personal conviction by becoming fully aware that—as Guru Rinpoche said—there is not even a pinhead of true happiness in samsara.

This conviction arises based on valid logic and reasoning. Therefore, the renunciation that we develop based on this is stable and no longer subject to fluctuations according to our mood that lead us to renounce one day and forget everything the following day. This disillusionment is the basis for enlightened mind that aspires to liberation and makes that its goal.

The state of mind that leads us to naturally give up samsara arises based on certain knowledge of its true nature. Attachment to temporary well-being—pleasant sensations that are enjoyable in the beginning but which transform into suffering when they reach their end—weakens. The lessening of attachment is a sign that renunciation is developing.

Renunciation is the source of countless benefits—most notably that of reducing our attachment to samsaric phenomena. It is the basis of all Buddhist practice, including the Dzogchen and Mahamudra practices known as superior, which cannot be accomplished correctly without renunciation.

When we have firmly established a basis of renunciation, we truly engage upon the path toward liberation by following the example of the accomplished beings of the past: bodhisattvas, panditas, mahasiddhas, etc. There is no other way to achieve this.

In the domain of Buddhist practice, we cannot invent another path, as we can with worldly things—saying, for example, "I have an idea! I am going to start a new business!" In the context of the Buddha's teaching, this cannot be done because the perfect path that leads to liberation is the only one that can give us this result.

Shakyamuni Buddha was born in Lumbini, in the realm of Kapilavastu. As a royal prince, he possessed immense riches and enjoyed a very luxurious life.

One day, he left the palace and went for a walk in the city. He encountered a sick person, an elderly person, and the corpse of someone who had just died. He was stunned by the experience and asked his attendant, "Does this happen to everyone? Will I also fall ill, get old, and die?"

His attendant replied, "Yes, that is the case. Even you, who will be a powerful king, will get old. One day, you will fall ill and die."

This deeply troubled the prince. In this way, he became aware that these types of suffering—old age, sickness, and death—are inevitable in this world. Natural renunciation arose within him.

The instant that the Buddha—at that time called Siddhartha—recognized impermanence, he wished right then to totally abandon samsara. As he led a princely life, he lacked nothing—in comparison, we have many more preoccupations—but the Buddha nevertheless chose to renounce everything in order to undertake the authentic path of liberation to accomplish the benefit of beings. He became a renunciant and continued on the path until he reached liberation and then enlightenment.

Shakyamuni Buddha himself, the founding father of Buddhism, used renunciation as a motor to move forward on the path to liberation and, in the end, to attain Buddhahood. Seeing the suffering that pervades samsara, he decided to give up his possessions and position to become a renunciant.

The first two seals contain the explanations of samsara's characteristics:

- All conditioned phenomena are impermanent by nature.
- All contaminated phenomena are suffering by nature.

Our task is to reflect on these two phrases and to integrate them until we are personally convinced of their truth.

The term *impermanence* means that everything in samsara changes from moment to moment. Well-being and happiness are temporary; when they cease, their disappearance gives way to suffering. Samsara's nature is unsatisfactory. There is no ultimate happiness in this condition.

Shakyamuni Buddha understood the impermanence and suffering that characterize samsara, and so he decided to give up worldly life and follow the path until enlightenment. Once he had fully accomplished the path, he taught the Dharma for the benefit of beings and explained these first two seals.

He was the first to undertake this path, but other accomplished masters who came later followed this same path. For example, Shantideva (c. 685–763 C.E.) and Atisha (982–1054 C.E.) were also born into royal families and renounced all of their possessions. They gave up their wealth to dedicate themselves to the same path that leads to liberation, and they traversed the various levels of accomplishment of the bodhisattvas. Both are considered to be remarkable Buddhist masters of the Mahayana and Tantrayana. Reading their biographies helps us to develop confidence, devotion, and courage. Their life stories are inspiring and beneficial in that they are examples that we can apply in our own lives and practice.

Guru Rinpoche (Padmasambhava), another master of note, was not born of a human womb, but rather appeared spontaneously upon a lotus flower. He was adopted by King Oddiyana and became the heir to the throne. Nevertheless, he gave up all this power and wealth to become a simple renunciant.

The majority of the great practitioners or mahasiddhas of the past came from wealthy families, and yet they renounced all worldly activities to follow the path of the yogi, which was at times a bit crazy—as in the case of Virupa, who held back the sun.

A great number of accomplished beings have followed the same path toward liberation, and it is this path that we too can follow. It is not necessary to take monastic vows to obtain liberation. The key lies in generating authentic renunciation of samsara.

The phrase "all contaminated phenomena are suffering by nature" means that everything we encounter in samara is unsatisfactory by nature. Renunciation does not refer to the suffering of suffering or the suffering of change. Renouncing samsara solely on the basis of these two categories does not constitute authentic renunciation. As we have previously discussed, even animals are capable of this. No animal wishes to suffer. Animals naturally seek to avoid the suffering of suffering, and they do not wish for circumstances in which their well-being comes to an end, either. Authentic renunciation arises when we are capable of recognizing the three types of suffering, and, most notably, the third—"all-pervasive suffering," also called "suffering in formation, moment after moment" and "omnipresent suffering," which is inherent in the simple fact of being born in samsara.

It is only due to subtle understanding of samsara's nature and the three forms of suffering that we can develop true renunciation. The profound wish to free oneself from all suffering arises simultaneously with renunciation.

The Root of Suffering

Understanding the origin or the cause of suffering is an essential part of the process that leads to disillusionment regarding samsara (based on knowledge of its unsatisfactory nature). Therefore, it is useful to ask oneself:

> Where does suffering come from?
> Did someone create it?
> Does it come from a creator god?
> Does it arise based on causes external to itself?
> Does it arise based on itself?
> Does it appear without a cause?

Reflection on these questions allows us to understand that suffering arises based on specific causes and conditions whose nature corresponds with the type of suffering they bring about. The origin of suffering is our karma: the acts we carry out. Karma results in our experiencing afflictive emotions; there lies the true cause of unhappiness.

An analysis of karma and afflictive emotions reveals that their appearance occurs based on a mistaken perspective that attributes true existence and inherent reality to the self. Afflicted states, karma, and, in turn, all of the suffering based on these things occurs due to this misunderstanding.

Since beginningless time, we apprehend our aggregates incorrectly—attributing true reality to them. We confuse them with an *I* that we conceive of as existing in and of itself. All of our desires arise based on this misunderstanding. "I want to be happy." "I need this." "I need that." We always want more to satisfy this *I*.

In an interdependent way, the conception of this *I* leads to the conception of *others.* The concepts of self and others are mutually dependent. On this basis, we develop strong attachment to our own self, this *I*, and we experience attachment or aversion toward others. Influenced by these two opposite notions, we act—thus generating karma, which results in diverse experiences of suffering.

As Chandrakirti said in the *Madhyamakavatara:*[24]

> *Beings think "I" at first, and cling to self;*

---

24 Chandrakirti, Jamgon Mipham, Padmakara Translation Group. *Introduction to the Middle Way: Chandrakirti's Madhyamakavatara*. Boston: Shambhala Publications, 2002, p. 59.

They think of "mine" and are attached to things.
Thus they turn helplessly as buckets on a waterwheel,
And to compassion for such beings I bow down![25]

First, we conceive of our own aggregates as though they have an inherent existence. Then, we take them to be an *I* that we become deeply attached to. Automatically, ideas of ownership (*mine*) and needs related to this *I* arise. Our attachment reinforces itself in this way and, as it grows stronger, transforms into greed and pushes us to act. The acts we carry out create karmic imprints that cause us to be reborn in samsara.

We can compare the self-perpetuating cycle of existences to an old-fashioned waterwheel with earthen buckets. As the wheel turns, the buckets on top go down to later rise up again, while those below rise up to later go down.

We carry out acts of various natures—virtuous and non-virtuous—based on attachment and greed. Virtuous acts allow us to be reborn in higher realms, but when the karma for this condition runs out, we return to the lower realms. In this way, we are endlessly reborn in different locations in the cycle—sometimes in happy circumstances, sometimes in unhappy circumstances.

The single root of all problems and suffering in samsara lies in this conception of an *I*. Therefore, we can ask ourselves:

> What is this *I*?
> Does it really exist?
> Where is it?

The goal is to analyze and reflect on the existence or

---

25 Sentient beings who wander in samsara life after life.

nonexistence of what we perceive as something solid and real.

In contrast to other religions or philosophical schools, Buddhism does not accept the existence of either a supreme entity or an independently-arising *I*. After having generated a certain amount of renunciation and having committed to the path of liberation, the *I*'s lack of inherent existence is the primary focus of reflection.

Q&A

Question: I don't understand the expression "renounce samsara" because the act of renouncing or renunciation usually refers to something pleasurable or something that gives us a pleasant sensation. In terms of suffering, everyone is always trying to get away from it. Due to our frenetic quest for happiness in samsara, we experience suffering, so renouncing it seems logical and easy.

Answer: Renunciation does not consist in renouncing the most obvious forms of suffering, such as the suffering of suffering and the suffering of change. All beings, including animals, are capable of renouncing these, for—as we have discussed—no one seeks them out.

There is a great difference between *not desiring* and *renouncing*. It is one thing not to desire something, and it is another to completely renounce something. Renunciation implies greater intensity and force. We should not confuse not desiring something and renouncing it.

The word we translate into English as *renunciation* is the Tibetan word *nejung*. The two syllables that make up this word indicate the two necessary aspects for authentic renunciation: first, perception of the characteristics of samsara—most notably the existential suffering inherent in all existence, all beings, and all phenomena within samsara—and second, the realization that liberation is the sole means of escaping this suffering. It is necessary to recognize the true nature of samsara and to aspire to no longer remain here.

The masters explain that when we go through a difficult time—a problematic or painful situation—we easily say that we no longer want to remain in samsara and that we renounce it. This is a very temporary state of mind, not an authentic renunciation. Indeed, as soon as the situation changes a few days later, we completely forget about renunciation.

Question: Do we have difficulty renouncing samsara because we still believe that we can find happiness here?

Answer: Yes, it is very difficult to fully and definitively renounce samsara in an authentic way. Nevertheless, it is important to do so because this is what sets an unsure practitioner apart from an authentic practitioner. A practitioner who is sincere in this way no longer nurtures any illusions about samsara and no longer wishes to perpetuate their own way of functioning. Renunciation is the antidote to attachment.

Attachment is like super glue. We are always stuck in the many aspects of samsara. Developing true renunciation is not easy because we are attached to everything. One way to define samsara is being attached to the illusion that happiness exists in samsara.

Question: Isn't there a contradiction between renunciation of samsara and the attitude of a bodhisattva whose motivation is to come back and help beings?

Answer: There is no contradiction because the bodhisattvas have already renounced samsara. They are not reborn based on afflictive emotions or attachment to the cycle of existences, but due to love and compassion for all beings.

Bodhisattvas who have reached the *bhumis* can be born according to different causes. Some are reborn in samsara thanks to the strength of aspirations or wishes they have made in the past. Others return due to their positive karma and yet others by the power of their meditative absorption and their wisdom.

However, beginning-level bodhisattvas cannot be reborn in samsara based on their meditative absorption or wisdom, but rather due to the strength of their past wishes and prayers that reach maturity—"In the future, may I be reborn in samsara and be of benefit to countless beings so that they may obtain happiness and free themselves from suffering!"

Question: You said that meditating on impermanence is important. Are there certain rules to follow or should we work based on our own criteria?

Answer: Gampopa's text *The Jewel Ornament of Liberation* explains this meditation very well and presents all the various points. This text is very useful because it is quite concise, and it lists all the essential elements without leaving any out. The analytical meditation consists in reading and reflecting upon the explanations while analyzing each point.

If we do not have access to this text, the simple reminder that outer objects and ourselves are impermanent is also a meditation.

In the first part of *The Preliminary Practices*,[26] the second sentence of one of the prayers covers impermanence:

> *This world and all it contains are transitory;*
> *Most especially, the life of beings is as fragile as a bubble*
>   *upon water.*
> *The moment of death is uncertain, and when it arrives,*
>   *we are then no more than a corpse.*
> *As the Dharma is what benefits us, let us practice it*
>   *with ardor.*

The preliminary practices refer to two things: the ordinary or common preliminary practices and the extraordinary preliminary practices.

The common preliminary practices consist of four reflections to carry out. The first focuses on the difficulty of obtaining a perfect human existence and the second on impermanence and death.

---

26 *Les pratiques préliminaires* [*The Preliminary Practices*]. Montchardon: Montchardon Diffusion, 2002, p.3.

III. All Phenomena Are Empty and Devoid of Inherent Existence

This sentence means that phenomena do not have the reality that we attribute to them; they do not truly exist.

Analysis of Inner Phenomena: The *I* and the Aggregates

From the point of view of the common vehicle, not a single phenomenon exists outside of the five aggregates. The point is to understand that the five aggregates are empty of inherent existence and, therefore, they cannot constitute a support for the existence of an *I*. Nevertheless, it is on the basis of these five aggregates that we develop a self that we feel to be truly present.

The Identification of *I* with the Aggregates

The first step is to examine whether or not the *I* and the aggregates are really the same thing.

As Nagarjuna says:

If the I and the aggregates are the same thing, then, in this case, there are several I. For the aggregates are plural, while the I is perceived as a singular entity—independent and unique.

There are five aggregates:
- Forms
- Sensations
- Distinctions
- Formations
- Consciousness

If the five aggregates and the *I* are identical, logically, there are also five *I*, or five entities. However, this does not agree with our conception.

Furthermore, if we analyze the aggregates, we can observe that each of them can be subdivided into numerous parts or aspects. Therefore, there should be as many *I* as there are aspects of each aggregate.

In addition, an *I* that is identical to the aggregates should be impermanent, which is contradictory to the immutable perception that we have of it. The aggregates are indeed dependent phenomena, and, therefore, impermanent. They depend on causes and conditions to appear.

Thus, it is not logical to believe in the existence of a permanent and autonomous *I*—in other words, one that does not depend on anything other than itself to exist—that is also transitory and relies on other causes and conditions outside itself to exist! The contradiction is obvious.

Shakyamuni Buddha and Chandrakirti, in his text the *Madhyamakavatara,* use the example of a chariot to demonstrate that the *I* has no inherent existence. The purpose of this example is to analyze the chariot according to a seven-step reasoning that also applies to the examination of the *I*. So, let us examine this ancient, horse-drawn car and ask ourselves:

What is the chariot?

Is the wheel the chariot?

Is the axle the chariot?

Various different parts make up a chariot, so:

What is the chariot itself?

Is it one of the pieces? If not, where is it?

We realize that neither the wheels, nor the axle, nor the cabin make up the chariot itself and that we cannot find the chariot in any of its individual parts.

Is the chariot the shape of all its parts or perhaps its color?

It is obvious that it cannot be reduced to one or the other.

Does the chariot then exist in the assembly of its parts?

This is not the case either.

This analysis leads us to the conclusion that what we call *chariot* cannot be found in any of the aspects mentioned. As such, it does not exist anywhere in the manner in which we conceive of it.

The idea is to apply this same reasoning to the aggregates—that is, to analyze the location of this *I* that we conceive of as auto-existent within the aggregates. We consider each of the aggregates in turn:

Is the *I* the aggregate of form?

Is it the aggregate of sensations, etc.?

Is it the shape of the aggregates?

Is it the collection of the aggregates?

At the end of this analysis, we come to the conclusion that the *I* cannot be found in any of these aspects. It abides neither in the interior nor the exterior of the aggregates. It does not exist as a permanent, independent entity such as we conceive of it[27].

One day in ancient India, a king went to visit an arhat, who addressed him in this way, "Where are you from? How did you get here?"

The king replied, "I came from a far-off country to visit you, and I came in a horse-drawn carriage."

The arhat then asked him, "Where is the carriage?"

The king pointed to it, but the arhat asked again, "Where exactly? You have not answered me correctly. Is the wheel the carriage? Is the axle the carriage? Is the shape the carriage? Is the color the carriage? Is the collection of these things the carriage? Where do we find the carriage?"

---

27 To clarify this point, we can also mention a segment from the ninth chapter of Mipham Rinpoche's book known as the *Kejuk* in Tibetan (mkhas 'jug) and translated into English as *Gateway to Knowledge* (Mipham Rinpoche, *Gateway to Knowledge, Vol. 4.* Hong Kong: Rangjung Yeshe Publications, 2002. P. 41.). This text pursues the analysis of the chariot in a more precise manner to show, in detail, how we assign an *I* to a collection of elements in the same way that we apply the label or term *chariot*, for example, to a whole made up of various elements.

1. The chariot is not identical to its wheels or any other of its individual parts.
2. It is also not completely different than its parts.
3. Therefore, the parts and the "possessor" of the parts do not possess each other.
4. The "possessor" of these parts cannot be found within them.
5. The parts, such as the wheels, etc., cannot be found to exist inside the chariot that they are part of.
6. The assemblage of the parts has no existence outside the parts themselves.
7. The appearance of the assemblage does not have the slightest existence outside of the parts themselves.

This analysis in seven points shows that it is impossible to find a true chariot that is the possessor of the different parts that constitute it. Thus, we understand that the chariot is only a conceptual designation applied to an assemblage of its own components. When we analyze the *I* using the seven steps of this reasoning, and we realize that it is only a simple label stuck onto a collection of different aggregates, we understand that it has no true existence.

Through his questions, the arhat was, in fact, giving the king a direct instruction on emptiness.

In general, reflecting on objects' absence of inherent existence is very beneficial, but in the context of Buddhist practice, it is also essential to analyze our own aggregates' or *I*'s absence of inherent existence.

The aggregates, as their name suggests, are a collection. They are not singular entities. Whether it is in Sanskrit (*skandha*), in Tibetan (*pungpo*), or in English, the term designates the unification of multiple elements. Therefore, an aggregate is, in part, the association of the four elements—air, fire, water, and earth—and, in part, the unification of various causes and conditions. The aggregates constitute the result of the combination of this collection of elements.

An analysis of the way that we conceive of the *I* allows us to understand that we apprehend it as a singular entity. Indeed, we do not perceive it as plural, but as one, independent, and permanent.

If the aggregates are, by nature, impermanent and made up of the association of various elements, then where is the *I*—since, by definition, it does not exist in the aggregates?

One of Shakyamuni Buddha's sutras says this on the subject:

> *This mistaken conception of I*
> *As being self-existing,*
> *Like a demon,*
> *Only serves to constantly harm us.*

This reflection allows us to become aware that the *I* does not exist as such. In the same way that we apply the label *chariot* to a collection of parts, we apply the label *I* to the aggregates. The *I* is only a designation that we impute to a collection of elements.

Shantideva states in the *Bodhicaryavatara*:

> *If all the violence that occurs in the world,*
> *All the fear and suffering,*
> *Arise from the attachment to me,*
> *Then what must I do to this demon?*

In this stanza, he explains that the mistaken concept of the *I* has caused us great difficulty since beginningless time without our being aware of it. Therefore, we should take advantage of the opportunity we have today and use our intelligence to understand that this has always been the cause of our problems.

Without this understanding, we think that others or outer circumstances cause unhappiness when, in reality, it occurs based on this mistaken idea of ourselves. When we become aware of this, we must be courageous and seize the sword of superior discernment to vanquish this false idea. This discernment allows us to understand that the *I* is not the aggregates, that it does not exist independently, and that it is not a self-existing entity like we believe it to be.

The Identification of the *I* with a Name

In general, when someone asks us who we are, we always respond with our name.

If someone asks me, "Who are you?" I reply, "I am Ngedön."

Ngedön is my name, but in reality, I am not a name. The identification with our names is the source of confusion.

If the *I* were the name, this would mean that when we were in our mother's belly and we did not yet have a name, the *I* did not exist either.

Several contradictions arise based on this identification. Since we receive our name after our birth, it is absurd to think that we are this name.

The Identification of the *I* with the Sensory Organs

We can use an example to explain this point. If someone asks us, "Can you see this teacup?" we will probably reply with, "Yes, we can see it."

However, in reality, we cannot see the teacup. Our eyes see it, but we, *ourselves*; do not see it.

If we follow this reasoning further, we can say that our eyes do not see the teacup either, but, rather, our visual consciousness sees it.

As we have always been accustomed to this type of confusion, it is difficult for us to be able to see reality as it is. We continue to fool our minds and to remain in the illusion of samsara by attributing reality to something that does not belong to it. In addition, we are unable to perceive what is true or real.

Identification of the *I* with the Sensations

We experience the *I* as an inner sensation, but it is not this either. There are different types of sensations. They can be pleasant, unpleasant, or neutral. Here, we can apply the same reasoning as before. There are numerous sensations, while we perceive the *I* as being individual. Therefore, they cannot be the same thing. A singular phenomenon and a plural phenomenon are not identical.

Furthermore, sensations are impermanent. They change, never remaining the same. If the sensation is impermanent, and the *I* is a sensation, then the *I* must also be changing and impermanent, but this does not correspond with the vision we have of it.

Knowing that all phenomena are empty of any inherent existence is essential for a Buddhist practitioner who wishes to attain liberation. This knowledge particularly develops through the analysis of our aggregates and the entity that we call *I*.

In the Mahayana vehicle, the absence of existence applies to all phenomena—both inner phenomena, like the aggregates, and outer phenomena, like objects. This nature of all things is not reserved for samsaric phenomena; it also includes the phenomena related to nirvana. Therefore, we can see that the aggregates are not empty of existence while, elsewhere, other phenomena exist that are not. Emptiness nature is the nature of all phenomena.

In the *Madhyamakavatara*, Chandrakirti explains that the Buddha told of two types of absence of inherent existence or two types of emptiness in order to help beings free themselves from suffering.

- The absence of inherent existence of phenomena
- The absence of inherent existence of the individual

In order to understand the absence of inherent existence of the individual or of the *I*, it is necessary to reflect and meditate using the same reasoning given in the example of the chariot—in other words by looking for where this *I* is located. Understanding the absence of inherent existence of outer phenomena relies on other types of reasoning.

Analysis of Outer Phenomena

There are five different forms of reasoning called the five Madhyamaka lines of reasoning. The most notable explanations are those of Nagarjuna, in the *Mulamadhyamakakarika*,[28] Aryadeva, in *The Four Hundred Stanzas*,[29] and Chandrakirti, in the *Madhyamakavatara*.[30] We can also find more concise explanations in the ninth chapter of Shantideva's *Bodhicharyavatara*, which focuses on transcendent knowledge. I advise you to use one of these texts as a reference and study the five lines of reasoning.

The Mistaken Separation Between the Subject that Perceives and the Perceiving Object

This refers to the duality that leads us to impute a reality to outer objects. Our confused mind adopts a false vision of outer phenomena and creates a duality. It distinguishes a subject that perceives as well as perceived objects, thus creating a separation between the perceiving *I* and the perceived outer phenomena. Furthermore, it attributes a reality to these outer phenomena.

Let us consider an example. We perceive a teacup placed on a table as solid matter. Due to strong habits an-

---

28　Garfield, Jay F., Nāgārjuna. *The Fundamental Wisdom of the Middle way: Nāgārjuna's Mūlamadhyamakakārikā*. New York: Oxford University Press, Inc., 1995.

29　Āryadeva, Gyel-tsap, Ruth Sonam, Sonam Rinchen Geshe. *Āryadeva·s Four Hundred Stanzas on the Middle Way: with Commentary by Gyel-tsap [bzhi brgya pa'i rnam bshad legs bshad snying po]*. Ithaca: Snow Lion Publications, 2008.

30　Chandrakirti, Jamgon Mipham, Padmakara Translation Group. *Introduction to the Middle Way: Chandrakirti's Madhyamakavatara*. Boston: Shambhala Publications, 2002.

chored within us since beginningless time, we perceive this object as real, solid, and truly existing. However, if the teacup were truly imbued with these characteristics, every person that perceives it should perceive its solidity and immutable existence just as we do. However, this is not the case. Accomplished beings, such as Milarepa, can move their hand through the teacup without meeting any obstacle. Furthermore, teachings explain that beings in the bardo can likewise cross through matter without any resistance.

If the teacup is self-existing, solid and permanent, we should all perceive it in the same way, but this is not the case, as certain forms of evidence show. The existence or permanence that we attribute to a phenomenon is not inherent to it.

The conclusion we seek to reach is that all outer objects are empty of inherent existence in the same way, and, in this way, they resemble an illusion or the images of a dream.

All Outer Phenomena Are Like the Images of a Dream

We can dream about different things: an immense mountain, an ocean, etc., and we know that these dream images include neither reality nor solidity. If this were not the case, our dream mountain would fill up and even overflow our house. If it were real, how could our bedroom contain it?

Even if our dream perceptions are not real, our dreams can provoke sensations and emotions. If the dream is pleasant, we experience pleasant sensations. On the contrary, if it is a nightmare, we feel fear. When we are awake, our perceptions function no differently. Even if nothing that we perceive is real, our dream perception brings about pleasant and unpleasant experiences for us. We become involved in these perceptions. We seek to prolong them or to reject them. We act on this basis and then experience the consequences of our acts. In reality, all of this mechanism occurs in our minds.

In short, it is important to understand that outer objects do not have their own, true nature. This is why we refer to them as unborn, which means that they never began an existence. However—from the perspective of relative truth—due to specific causes and conditions, we perceive various phenomena, and we attribute a solid reality to them. Understanding interdependence allows us to discover that the field of perception manifests based on the meeting of causes and conditions.

The explanation of subtle impermanence showed us that change occurs from moment to moment and that, ultimately, an instant itself has neither appearance nor cessation. This is the true nature of phenomena on a subtle level.

We must understand that—by nature—all outer phenomena have no inherent existence and are not true entities.

The Inseparability of the Object's Appearance and Its Emptiness

Nevertheless, we perceive outer objects. In fact, the empty nature of the object and its manifestation coexist.

The Buddha states in *The Heart Sutra:*[31]

---

31   sangs rgyas bcom ldan 'das. *bcom ldan 'das ma shes rab kyi pha rol du phyin pa'i snying po' [The Heart Sutra]*. Biollet: Kundreul Ling, Undated.

Form is emptiness; emptiness is form.
Form is no other than emptiness;
Emptiness is no other than form.

The point is to understand what it means that outer objects' manifestation and their emptiness are insepa-rable. When we pour milk into water, the two liquids become inseparable. This is not the type of inseparabil-ity in question here. Indeed, even if we pour milk into water, these two elements remain distinct entities that can be separated. According to Nagarjuna and Atisha, this is not a total inseparability, for there is a bird able to consume only the milk in a mixture of milk and water—leaving the water behind. Therefore, we cannot consid-er this mixture to be truly inseparable because the two entities can be split apart with the appropriate methods.

Therefore, it is necessary to understand the insepa-rability of an object's manifestation and its emptiness in a different way—like that of a fire and its heat, which is its nature. These two aspects are truly indivisible. The very presence of fire indicates the presence of heat. It is not possible to separate the hot nature of fire, or the fire, from the heat.

We can understand the inseparability of an object's manifestation and its nature—emptiness—in this way, as the third seal states: all phenomena are empty and devoid of inherent existence. Full conviction in this no-tion is the fruit of personal experience, which can only occur through deep reflection on this seal.

The process is the same for all Buddhist meditation: the goal is to personally arrive at a profound conviction without which we cannot undertake the path of libera-tion. Thanks to the written teachings, oral instructions, and our own reasoning, we reach the personal conviction that all phenomena are empty of inherent existence.

This discernment—with its understanding of emptiness—acts as the sole antidote to our mistaken perception concerning the *I* and outer objects, which we conceive of as independent, truly existing entities. These perceptions constitute the very root of samsara and the origin of our suffering and our problems. Virtuous actions and beneficial practices allow us to accumulate positive karmic imprints, but they cannot uproot the mistaken conception that we maintain of reality. Only discernment that apprehends emptiness is useful in this regard.

Therefore, understanding emptiness—*shunyata*, also called the absence of inherent existence—is key.

Theravada vehicle teachings discuss the absence of inherent existence of the *I*. Mahayana and Vajrayana teachings also include the absence of inherent existence of outer phenomena in addition to that of the *I*.

Thus the subject is twofold: the emptiness of the *I* and that of outer phenomena.

The application of the Tantric practices of the Vajrayana requires recognition of these two aspects. Indeed, when we carry out a *yidam* practice, which includes various visualizations, maintaining the perspective of emptiness is essential. The point is to be conscious of the empty nature of the presence established during our meditation practice. Without this understanding, Vajrayana practice is ineffective because it eliminates neither our ego nor the mistaken conceptions of the *I* and the reality of outer phenomena that we maintain. Tantrayana[32] practice must be founded on discernment

---

32   Tantrayana is a synonym for Vajrayana. See glossary.

that apprehends emptiness.

Once we have integrated this point, we meditate, and we focus on understanding the absence of inherent existence of all phenomena.

The Method for Meditating on the Four Seals of the Dharma

There are three points to this method.

Meditation Posture

When we meditate, we adopt the seven points of *vajra* posture. The most important is to keep the back straight and the gaze in the correct position. There are different explanations concerning the gaze according to the meditation practice in question. In the context of *shine* meditation (*shamata* in Sanskrit)—the meditation of mental calm—we focus the gaze slightly downward. We look at a point roughly four finger-lengths from the tip of our nose. At floor level, this corresponds with a place approximately a yard from where we are seated. If we meditate on *shunyata*, emptiness, the instructions tell us to keep our gaze straight in front of us.

In the context of Mahamudra or Maha Ati meditation, we direct our gaze slightly upward.

Generating Renunciation

When we sit down to meditate, we begin by turning our minds toward renunciation by reflecting on the first two seals that describe the characteristics of samsara:

All conditioned phenomena are impermanent by nature.

All contaminated phenomena are suffering by nature.

This reflection gives rise to natural disillusionment and also inspires us to commit to the path of liberation.

Commitment to the Path

The path refers to the third seal: all phenomena are empty and devoid of inherent existence. When we commit to the path, we meditate on the absence of inherent existence of all phenomena and on subtle impermanence, which leads us to realize emptiness. In this way, we cut the root of samsara—the two mistaken ideas of an independent existence of the *I* and a true reality of phenomena.

By eradicating these two mistaken concepts, we also eliminate the development of afflictive emotions and karma. We put an end to suffering by wiping out its source. What is left? A state of absolute peace.

IV. Nirvana Is a State of Absolute Peace.

When we eliminate the causes of suffering—afflictive emotions and karma—we put a definitive end to suffering and, thus, attain a state of absolute peace, joy, and well-being. This state is totally free of dissatisfaction or unhappiness and is perfectly stable and continuous.

It does not even slightly resemble the type of well-being we may experience now, which is a mental state similar to a weather report. Sometimes we might say, "Today, I feel good," but the following day, "Today, everything is terrible," and the day after that, "I feel alright again."

Our current mental state fluctuates constantly. The term *nirvana*, which refers to the joy outside of samsara, literally means *to go beyond suffering*. The syllable *nir* refers to suffering and evokes the image of a very dense jungle.

Our Current State: The Jungle

The situation we currently find ourselves in resembles a dense jungle where the overgrown trees and vegetation mask the sun and sky and cut off all escape routes. We feel overwhelmed by a sensation of desolation, despair, and fear that prevents us from breathing, and we are incapable of moving forward due to wild animals—dangerous lions and tigers or venomous spiders and snakes—and vines and branches that cut off our movements. Fear-filled sweat runs down our bodies and our sole thought is, "How am I going to get out of here? How can I get free from this situation?"

Samsara is like this dense jungle filled with dangers. Venomous creatures symbolize the afflictive emotions: attachment, pride, desire, anger, and jealousy. These emotions cause us harm every moment—bringing about suffering, problems, and hardships. Getting through this jungle and getting out of our current situation remains difficult.

In the term nirvana, the first syllable, *nir*, describes this type of perilous situation. The second syllable, *vana*, means *beyond*. Thus, we can translate nirvana by *to go beyond our situation of suffering*.

Escaping the Jungle

Let us imagine that the person trapped in the jungle finally manages to escape and to reach a peaceful, green clearing. Now free from all danger, they can at last relax and enjoy the cool, fresh air. Nirvana is like this clearing: a state of absolute peace and happiness.

This state is perfectly stable. Attaining it means never again being reborn in samsara, nor experiencing suffering, because the afflictive emotions—the primary cause of unhappiness—are no longer present. Reaching nirvana means being safe from all danger and thus experiencing a stable and perfect state of peace and joy.

When we attain nirvana, we also actualize the countless qualities inherent to Buddhahood, such as boundless love and compassion and enlightened activity. These qualities are naturally present within us and allow us to help all beings in a way that is inconceivable to us at present.

It is important not to envision nirvana as an outer location—somewhere far off where we arrive after a long, laborious journey that requires great effort and preparation. It is, rather, an inner state that we realize. Indeed, the instant we dissipate the mistaken conception of an *I* and the belief in outer phenomena's inherent existence, afflictive emotions and karma exhaust themselves and a state of absolute peace arises.

Some people believe that we cannot attain nirvana during the course of our lives, and can only do so after death. This is not the case, and taking action geared in this direction after death is difficult. Instead, the opportunity is present in this very life. Starting now, we have the chance to progress toward this goal.

Once dead, it is more difficult to act and we do not know what will happen. Because our future lives depend on our present conduct, we cannot know, now, what is to come. The moment of death is like a dark passageway whose end we cannot make out. The opportunity to give up our illusions regarding samsara is present beginning in this life, thanks to our human existence, which allows us to carry out beneficial actions. This perfect state is accessible to us starting now.

In a way, we find ourselves close to the border that separates samsara from nirvana. We have not yet quite reached this border, but integrating the teaching on the four seals of the Dharma allows us to move closer. When we arrive at the border, only our determination will decide whether we cross it or return the same way that we came from. If we go backwards, we will begin the same story again: a repetitive cycle that leads us upward one moment and downward another moment.

Having presently obtained a perfect human rebirth endowed with positive conditions, we can put these conditions to good use to edge closer to the boundary and cross it. We can even say that, as we have the ability and discernment necessary to distinguish that which is beneficial from that which is harmful, we must put to use the great opportunity that we have today.

Although beings who have attained a human existence are numerous, those who are able to distinguish the beneficial from the harmful are rare. Among this category, those who apply this knowledge are rarer still, and those who practice with authentic renunciation toward the goal of liberation are even fewer. Furthermore, the number of practitioners seeking this goal while keeping others in mind and expressing the wish, "May they obtain liberation and enlightenment for the benefit of all!" is even more miniscule.

Today, we have the conditions—both inner and outer—to put to work that which leads to liberation. Therefore, we must take note of the precious opportunity available to us. Meditating on impermanence with this correct appreciation for our situation is important because contemplating the ephemeral nature of our circumstances will inspire us not to waste any time.

Reflecting on these four seals, meditating on their meaning, and acting in accordance with them contributes to accomplishing something meaningful in our lives.

Q&A

Question: Could we say that a bodhisattva is close to crossing this border?

Answer: There are different types of bodhisattvas and many levels of bodhisattvas. Which are you referring to?

Question: I'm speaking about bodhisattvas in general.

Answer: If a beginning bodhisattva generates love and compassion for all beings based on renunciation, then not only is this bodhisattva approaching the border, they can cross it.

Question: When we prepare for renouncing samsara after having meditated a great deal on this point, what should we do with the suffering that arises? Should we ignore it? Not accord it any importance? Try to avoid it? Or should we simply leave it aside and ask ourselves one of the three questions related to the root of this suffering?

Answer: To begin with, everything depends on the time necessary for generating authentic renunciation. Therefore, this depends on the individual. If we manage to see the nature of samsara clearly, this renunciation will arise naturally, but nothing is predetermined. The most important point concerning renouncing samsara is determination. We must be courageous, enthusiastic, and perseverant. Most of the time, we lack the necessary courage to go in the direction of renunciation and all that it implies.

Ignoring our suffering is pointless, and all it will get us is more unhappiness. We abide in samsara, which is suffering. It is useless to pretend otherwise. However, we can go in the direction of renunciation. If developing complete renunciation remains out of our reach, we can, nevertheless, progress gradually according to our own ability.

In fact, it is a question of accepting suffering. The first step is recognizing it. Then, we become aware that our own karma—past beneficial and harmful actions—brings about the situation we are in. Understanding that our past actions lead to our current circumstances helps us accept our situation. This understanding allows us to experience suffering more peacefully, which allows us to undergo hardships with less anxiety, preoccupation, and intensity.

Knowing that all situations of suffering arise based on our own actions, we understand that if we wish to avoid future suffering, then we need to be more conscientious about what we do. Beneficial actions always lead to positive experiences and harmful actions always result in unhappy experiences. Once we understand the law of karma, it is up to us to act accordingly.

From a worldly point of view, carrying out virtuous actions consists in understanding that our current beneficial actions allow us to avoid future situations of suffering and to create positive conditions in this life and subsequent lives.

Question: Is it at the very instant that we realize emptiness that we attain nirvana?

Answer: Yes.

Question: By accepting the non-existence of the I, how does Buddhism define who or what is reborn?

Answer: The one who takes rebirth in samsara is the one who mistakenly perceives the existence of the *I*.

Question: That's not what I was referring to. Once we have accepted that the I does not exist, how does Buddhism define the essence of the individual? What is left after the I is eradicted?

Answer: This is a very vast theme, but we can summarize it by saying that the I is imputed to a fundamental consciousness called the *alayavijnana* in Sanskrit. If the *I* does not exist, we call what remains the fundamental consciousness or base consciousness.

By eliminating the conception of an *I*, we arrive at the pure essence: the true nature of mind or *tathagatagarbha*, the Buddha nature present within each of us.

Question: In certain teachings, I have heard that samsara and nirvana have the same essence. In the practice I do, there is a prayer that reads, "I invoke my master so that I may liberate myself from the chains of samsara and nirvana." What does this other vision of nirvana correspond to?

Answer: Yes, we speak about this in the Mahayana teachings where it is said that we must attain this state beyond the two extremes of samsara and nirvana. In the Kagyü school, we call this state of realization Mahamudra. In this Nyingma school, it is Maha Ati, and in the Sakya school, it is the inseparability of samsara and nirvana. Perhaps your question comes from there.

This refers to the third seal; which explains that the appearance and the emptiness of an object are inseparable. In other words, the perceived object and its nature are indivisible.

Appearance and emptiness refer to samsara and nirvana. Appearance is samsara; this is what we perceive. Emptiness is nirvana; this is the true nature of what we perceive. From the perspective of ultimate reality, these two aspects are inseparable.

What must we give up then? Our habitual perception of samsara. We need to stop maintaining attachment to the appearances that make up our world. The point is to give up the habit of judging samsaric appearances as being positive and thinking that they can make us happy. As such, the idea is not to give up appearances, but, rather, the opinion that we have of them. The goal is not to abandon the inseparability of form and emptiness, but to understand and recognize that appearance and emptiness are inseparable.

We are currently incapable of recognizing this indivisibility. Due to our ignorance, we delude ourselves, and we adopt an untrue vision of what surrounds us, which leads to our experiences of suffering.

The goal is to abandon this mistaken or false perception because it leads us to believe that phenomena have an inherent existence.

Question: When contaminated phenomena present themselves to us, how do we obtain the proper vision that allows us to recognize them?

Answer: We do not need to recognize them, for all phenomena that we perceive are contaminated phenomena. Why are they contaminated? Because they arise based on mistaken or false perception. This includes all of these phenomena that manifest based on afflictive emotions and karma. As such, the goal is to recognize and accept that all phenomena that we perceive are contaminated. If we are convinced of this, we will see that this contamination constitutes the root of suffering. The discernment we develop allows us not to forget and to see—from moment to moment—that all appearances that manifest are equally affected and perceived by mistaken vision. Therefore, we can apply the antidotes to counteract this way of seeing things.

Conclusion of the Teaching

We have now reached the end of the teaching on the four seals of the Dharma. I am happy to have been able to share these words and this important teaching from the Buddha. I hope that they will contribute to a better understanding of the Dharma.

The key point is to, first, develop beneficial motivation, then, to live in a respectful, harmonious way with those around us, and, last, to continue to learn and apply the Dharma—study and meditation practice go together.

I would like to thank all the precious qualified masters from the bottom of my heart for the blessing of their boundless kindness and supreme wisdom. I would also like to thank my close friends and students for their remarkable help and support in all situations.

I wrote all of the thoughts that came to my mind in this book without changing them. Due to this and to my lack of understanding and limited knowledge, it is possible that there are some errors. I pray to realized beings to excuse my contradictions, inconsistencies, or other mistakes.

May even the slightest beneficial activity or pure motivation arising based on this work contribute to peace in the world, give rise to *bodhicitta* and *mahakaruna*[33] in all beings, and also help all beings live free from the suffering of samsara!

---

33 *Mahakaruna*: great compassion

Dedication

May the sublime and precious bodhicitta arise
In all those within whom it has not yet arisen.
May it never diminish but always increase
In all those within whom it has already arisen!
May all beings have happiness!
May the lower realms empty forever
And may all of the prayers of the bodhisattvas
Be perfectly fulfilled!
Like space, earth,
And the other great elements,
May I support the lives of beings,
Limitless in number, in many different ways!
The infinite amount of beings
Fills all of space.
As far as their karma
And their negative emotions extend,
May my aspirations reach there as well.

Sarva Mangalam

Glossary

aggregates (the five): The aggregates are the unification or aggregation of numerous elements and diverse parts. The five aggregates are the aggregates of forms, sensations, distinctions, formations, and consciousness. The first refers to forms, and the four other refer to the mind. Together, they are the basis for self-grasping. By apprehending them as a single entity, we think that we truly exist as individuals. A more precise examination allows us to observe that the aggregate of forms—a body, for example, is not a single, real, and permanent entity, but rather the assemblage of numerous elements.

arhat: This term refers to *one who has vanquished afflictive emotions.* A practitioner who has realized the result of the listener or *pratekyabuddha* vehicle. They are liberated from samsara, but they have not yet attained the perfect enlightenment of a buddha.

Atisha Dipamkara (982–1054 C.E.): A great Indian master and scholar known in Tibet as Jowo Je, The Master. He was one of the most famous teachers of the Indian university Vikramashila. He was particularly well-versed in monastic discipline. He received teachings on *bodhicitta* from important masters, notably Suvarnadvipa (also called Dharmakirti or Serlingpa in Tibetan). During the last ten years of his life, he lived in Tibet, where he transmitted numerous teachings that revived the Dharma after a period of persecution. He greatly contributed to the translation of Buddhist texts into Tibetan. His most important work is the *Bodhipathapradipa, A Lamp for the Path to Enlightenment.*[34]

bhumi: Means *ground* or *level of realization* and refers to the different degrees of accomplishment of bodhisattvas on the spiritual path up until the perfect enlightenment of a Buddha. Teachings generally count ten bhumis.

bodhicitta: Enlightened (*bodhi*) mind (*citta*). Bodhicitta has two aspects: relative and absolute. The relative level concerns the aspiration to attain enlightenment for the benefit of all beings thanks to the practice of love and compassion and the six transcendent perfections or *paramitas* (generosity, ethics, patience, perseverance, meditative concentration, and wisdom) that are necessary to attain this objective. On an absolute level, bodhicitta refers to the direct perception of the true nature of all phenomena—ultimate reality.

---

34 Atisha. *Lamp for the Path to Enlightenment*. New York: Snow Lion Publications, 1997.

bodhisattva: A practitioner of the Mahayana vehicle; a being who has manifested enlightened mind and who progresses along the path toward enlightenment. The bodhisattva's goal is to attain Buddhahood in order to free all sentient beings in the six realms of samsara from suffering and to lead them to enlightenment.

causal relationship: Link or relationship between objects or phenomena. Buddhism describes two types of links or relationships between phenomena: either both phenomena are of the same nature or there is a link of cause and effect between them. As such, a virtuous or positive cause will always yield a virtuous or positive result, while a negative cause will always yield a negative result.

dharma **(Sanskrit):** *Chö* in Tibetan. Phenomenon. It also refers to the Buddha's teachings (in which case it is capitalized as a proper noun) and, in this case, it protects from the suffering of samsara. This usage also includes the meaning of correcting errors, as the Buddha's teaching allows us to avoid mistakes and negative actions of body, speech, and mind. It also constitutes the supreme path that leads to the excellent fruit: enlightenment. The *Dharma of the texts* is the transmission of the scriptural teachings and the *Dharma of realization* (or of the states of wisdom) is the fruit of the practice of the path. Even if the Dharma of realization is currently out of our reach, we can nevertheless easily access the Dharma of the texts, in other words the teaching of the Buddha's words.

dharmakaya: Absolute body, non-fabricated luminosity, or Buddha nature.

Dzogchen: The highest practice of the Nyingmapa tradition. It is also called Maha Ati—The Great Perfection.

enlightenment: The ultimate state of realization—that of a Buddha. For more on this theme, one can refer to the third Karmapa, Rangjung Dorje's text the *Nyingpo Tenpa*.

Gampopa (1079–1153 C.E.): Also known as Dhagpo Rinpoche or Dhagpo Lhaje. He was a disciple of Milarepa and one of the founding fathers of the Kagyü lineage. He is the author of numerous texts, including *The Precious Garland of the Sublime Path*, *The Jewel Ornament of Liberation*, and several texts on Mahamudra. In *The Jewel Ornament of Liberation*, a guidebook to the Mahayana Buddhist path, Gampopa brings together the Kadampa School's teachings on the gradual path with Mahamudra instructions from Milarepa. This work covers all aspects and all steps of a spiritual practitioner's progress, from their initial contact with the Dharma up through enlightenment.

Kadam: A school created by Drom Rinpoche, or Dromtenpa, in 1056 C.E. He was one of the four primary disciples of Atisha Dipamkara, whose teachings are the foundation for this school.

Kagyü: The lineage of oral transmission, one of the four principal schools of Tibetan Buddhism. The other traditions are the Nyingma School, Sakya School, and Gelug School. The founder of the school was Gampopa, disciple of Milarepa, disciple of Marpa the Translator, disciple of the Indian master Naropa, disciple of the Indian master Tilopa. Gampopa himself had four primary disciples including Düsum Khyenpa, who was the first Karmapa or first head of the Karma Kagyü lineage.

Karma: Action. It refers to the process of an act creating a cause that results in an effect. Each cause produces an effect similar to itself, and, inversely, each effect is the result of a prior corresponding cause.

Karuna: Compassion in Sanskrit. Compassion is the profound wish that all beings may become free from suffering and its causes. This virtue is central to all schools of Buddhism, particularly in the Mahayana and Tantrayana. We particularly develop this quality through meditation and extend it to all beings without restriction. In Mahayana Buddhism, compassion constitutes the necessary complement to wisdom and is an essential element for achieving complete enlightenment. Wisdom and compassion are the two wings of a bird that allow it to fly toward the island of enlightenment.

Lojong: Mind training. Training and study that allow one to develop enlightened mind, which makes up the bodhisattva's path. One of the most well-known practices for training on this path is the teaching by the Indian master Atisha Dipamkara titled *The Seven Points of Mind Training.*[35]

Maha Ati: Great Perfection. The highest level of practice in the Nyingma tradition.

---

35 Shamar Rinpoche, Braitstein, Lara E., Chekawa Yeshe Dorje. *The Path to Awakening: How Buddhism's Seven Points of Mind Training Can Lead You to a Life of Enlightenment and Happiness.* Harrison: Delphinium Books, 2014.

Mahamudra: Great Seal. The highest level of practice in the Kagyü tradition.

mahasiddha: Great accomplished one. A yogi who has obtained supreme realization.

Mahayana: Great vehicle or bodhisattva's vehicle. The entirety of the Buddha's teachings based on the sutras that explain the path a bodhisattva must follow to attain complete enlightenment or Buddhahood. Also called the causal vehicle.

Milarepa (1040–1123 C.E.): Famous Tibetan yogi, poet, and *mahasiddha*. He was among the most important disciples of Marpa and one of the founding fathers of the Kagyü lineage.

Nyingma: The oldest of the four schools of Tibetan Buddhism.

Padmasambhava: One who appeared from a lotus, also called the Second Buddha. He also goes by the name Guru Rinpoche (precious master). He spontaneously appeared from a lotus flower in the middle of a lake in the Oddiyana region. This Indian master allowed for the development of Buddhist teachings in Tibet and introduced the Tantric teachings there in the 8th century.

pandit: Scholar. Designation for the Indian scholars. In Tibet, the terms *khenpo* and *geshe* appear more often. In Buddhism, a scholar refers to a person endowed with nine specific qualities. The first three are the practice of study, reflection, and meditation that allow for the emergence of wisdom. The following three are discipline, kindness, and scholarship. The final three are the ability to teach, to compose texts, and to debate.

parinirvana: The death of a Buddha or accomplished Buddhist master in the Vajrayana.

principle of cause and effect: See *karma.*

vajra **posture:** Physical meditation posture described in seven points. It is also called Vairocana's posture.

samsara: See *six realms of samsara.*

sentient beings: Beings who are reborn within one of the six realms of samsara.

Shantideva (690–740 C.E.): An Indian master of royal descent and a member of the monastic university Nalanda. He is the author of several works, the most famous of which is the *Bodhicharyavatara.* All the schools of Buddhism have studied, commentated, and practiced this famous poem. This reference text is a guide for bodhisattvas.

six realms of samsara: The teachings represent samsara, also called the cycle of existences, with a continuously turning wheel that is divided into six worlds. There are three realms in the upper part of the wheel: the god realm, demigod realm, and human realm. There are three other realms in the lower part, referred to as the lower realms: the animal realm, the hungry ghost realm, and the hell realm. Sentient beings are reborn in one or another of these realms, life after life, according to the karmic imprints they have accumulated.

Tantrayana: Vehicle of the Tantras, also called the Mantrayana or Vajrayana. The entirety of the teachings based on the Tantras make up this vehicle, which allows one to progress rapidly on the path toward enlightenment for the benefit of beings. It is also referred to as the vehicle of result because the practitioner identifies with the result of the path—i.e. the qualities of Buddhahood as represented by a *yidam*—to progress. The Tantrayana is a branch of the great vehicle or Mahayana.

The Three Jewels: The Buddha, the Dharma, and the Sangha.

tonglen: Literally, giving and taking. A meditation practice consisting in giving others our merit and positive qualities while taking on their suffering. This practice is part of *lojong* (mind training toward enlightened mind) and, more specifically, constitutes mind training in relative *bodhicitta*.

vajra **song:** Also called a *doha*. A spontaneous song of realization expressed by accomplished beings who have a direct experience of the true nature of phenomena. The purpose of these songs is to help beings to attain the same accomplishment as the singer.

vehicle: In the context of Buddhism, this refers to a collection of teachings and methods to accomplish a spiritual path.

worldly action: Action carried out on the basis of belief in the real existence of an *I* and an *other*. This concerns actions contaminated by the afflictions (the five primary afflictions are desire-attachment, aversion, ignorance, jealousy, and pride), which occur within the six realms or worlds of samsara (thus, they are referred to as worldly).

yidam: A meditation divinity in advanced practices of Tantric Buddhism. *Yidams* are the manifestation of enlightened mind's qualities. We can compare the Buddha to the sun and the *yidam* to its rays.

Works Cited

Atisha. *Lamp for the Path to Enlightenment.* New York: Snow Lion Publications, 1997.

Āryadeva, Gyel-tsap, Ruth Sonam, Sonam Rinchen Geshe. *Āryadeva's Four Hundred Stanzas on the Middle Way: with Commentary by Gyel-tsap [bzhi brgya pa'i rnam bshad legs bshad snying po].* Ithaca, NY: Snow Lion Publications, 2008.

Buddha Shakyamuni, Conze Edward. *The Short Prajnaparamita Texts.* London: Luzac & Company Ltd., 1973.

Chandrakirti, Jamgon Mipham, Padmakara Translation Group. *Introduction to the Middle Way: Chandrakirti's Madhyamakavatara.* Boston: Shambhala Publications, 2002.

Choephel, David Karma, Ninth Karmapa, Wangchuk Dorje, Vasubandhu. *Jewels from the Treasury: Vasubhandu's Verses on the Treasury of Abhidharma And Its Commentary Youthful Play.* Woodstock: KTD Publications, 2012.

Gampopa, Erik Pema Kunsang. *The Precious Garland of the Sublime Path: The Oral Instructions of Lord Gampopa [lam mchog rin po che'i phreng ba].* Kathmandu: Rangjung Yeshe Publications, 1995.

Gampopa, Ani K. Trinlay Chödron, Khenchen Könchog Gyaltshen Rinpoche. *The Jewel Ornament of Liberation: The Wish-fulfilling Gem of the Noble Teachings [dam chos rin po che yid bzhin nor bu thar pa rin po che'i rgyan/].* New York: Snow Lion Publications, 1998.

Garfield, Jay F., Nāgārjuna. *The Fundamental Wisdom of the Middle way: Nāgārjuna's Mūlamadhyamakakārikā.* New York: Oxford University Press, Inc., 1995.

Mipham Rinpoche. *Gateway to Knowledge.* Hong Kong: Rangjung Yeshe Publications, 2002.

Kyabje Kangyur Rinpoche, Nagarjuna, Padmakara Translation Group. *Nagarjuna's Letter to a Friend [Suhrllekha].* Ithaca: Snow Lion Publications, 2005.

Patrul Rinpoche, Padmakara Translation Group. *The Words of My Perfect Teacher [rdzogs pa chen po klong chen snying tig gi sngon 'gro'i khrid yig kun bzang bla ma'i zhal lung zhes bya ba zhugs so].* Boston: Shambala Publications, 1999.

sangs rgyas bcom ldan 'das. *Bcom ldan 'das ma shes rab kyi pha rol du phyin pa'i snying po'* [*The Heart Sutra*]. Biollet: Kundreul Ling, Undated.

sangs rgyas bcom ldan 'das. *ched du brjod pa'i tshoms (Udānavarga)* [*The Chapters Stated with Intention*]. Publisher Unknown, Undated.

sangs rgyas bcom ldan 'das. *dran pa nye bar gzhag pa bzhi bstan pa,* [*The Sutra on Establishing Mindfulness*]. Biollet: Kundreul Ling, Undated.

Shantideva, Batchelor, Stephen. *A Guide to the Bodhisattva's Way of Life [Bodhisattvacharyavatara].* Dharamsala: Library of Tibetan Works and Archives (LTWA), 1992-1993.

Zangpo, Bengar Jampel *kar+ma pad bang phyug rdo rje. Sgrub brgyud rin po che'i phreng ba kar+ma kA tshang rtogs pa'i don brgyud las byung ba'i gsung dri ma me dpa rnams bkod nas ngag 'don rgyun khyer gyi rim pa 'phags lam bgrod pa'i shing rta* [*The Supplication to the Past Lineage of the Mahamudra*]. Biollet: Kundreul Ling, Undated.

Zangpo, Gyelse Thogme. "The 37 Practices of Bodhisattvas." Lotsawa House. https://www.lotsawahouse.org/tibetan-masters/gyalse-thogme-zangpo/37-practices-all-bodhisattvas. December 3, 2019.

Publishing finished
in January 2021 by Pulsio
Publisher Number: 4011
Legal Deposit: March 2021
Printed in Bulgaria